TAJIRIBA SPACES

The Solution to Sub-Optimal Outcomes

BY

GEOFFREYSON KHAMALA

Published By:

FOUNDATION

"Thinking for the Universe"

ISBN-13: 978-1508683292

ISBN-10: 1508683298

DEDICATION

I dedicate this book to thinking gurus, their admirers and critics worldwide.

TABLE OF CONTENTS

LIST OF ACRONYMS & ABBREVIATIONS

AKDN   -   Aga Khan Development Network

BCE   –   Before Common Era

CAR   -   Central African Republic

CE   -   Common Era

e.g.   -   For example

etc.   -   et cetera

i.e.   -   that is

ICANN   -   The Internet Corporation for Assigned Names

and Numbers

ILO   -   International Labour Organization

IMF   -   International Monetary Fund

NGOs   -   Non-Governmental Organizations

SAPs   -   Structural Adjustment Programmes

UN   -   United Nations

UN HABITAT-	United Nations Human Settlement Programme
UNDP	-	United Nations Development Programme
UNSC	-	United Nations Security Council
US	-	United States

PUBLICATIONS BY GEOFFREYSON KHAMALA

1. The Perfect Theory: A Complete Unified Description of the Universe (2014)

2. What is science? Science as an Adaptive Capacity (2014)

3. Is Science Religion? (2014)

4. Wither Globalization Enter Connectedness (2014)

5. The Ultimate Theory: The Perfect Description of the Universe (2015)

6. Tajiriba Spaces: The Solution to Sub-Optimal Outcomes (2015)

7. Zero Unemployment in Kenya: The Utility of Tajiriba Spaces (2015)

8. Reclaiming the Sahara: A Case for Universal Connectedness (2015)

ABSTRACT

Relatedness, the current structuring of the human society, determines resource optimality worldwide. The world has a resource underutilization/underinvestment/misapplication problem. Sub-optimal consequences are unfavourable results of identity politics and struggles and the subsequent inadequacy of opportunities for most people to positively utilize their adaptive capacities.

Relatedness apparently encourages competition along fault lines for power, resources and mating partners. Some of the major unfavorable outcomes include discrimination, mistrust and suspicion; unemployment; poverty; economic fluctuations; global terrorism; and identity conflicts and war.

Because of relatedness, most remote rural locations, urban slums and other peripheral geographical locations around the world are battling to cope with the lack of or poor infrastructure and planning.

To unleash the world's full potential, it is important to de-emphasis the now widespread identity triumphalist plot by embracing connectedness in order to scale up investments in physical infrastructure, to realize inclusive growth, and to diminish the meaning of borders.

Enterprise development in deprived locations throughout the world can help close the income opportunity gap. However, efforts to foster enterprise in some parts of the world frequently runs into whirlwinds since the private sector may be incapable or disinclined to absorb the infrastructural costs associated with establishing businesses in far-flung and often relatively less-profitable locations.

The presumption that government intervention can tackle market failures through public policy choices only holds when we pretend government failures don't happen. Yet evidence abounds showing commonness of non-market failures.

Recently we are witnessing situations in which market failures are combined with imperfection in government performance due in large part to the relatedness dilemma. Relatedness dilemma refers to coincident market failure and government failure arising from politics along fault lines. In such scenarios, the non-profit sector is obligated to support infrastructure investment to guarantee productivity, evenhanded growth and to facilitate the creation of new income opportunities.

Tajiriba Spaces (urbanized neighborhoods) represents an innovative mechanism for the non-profit sector to compliment government intervention and/or encourage more private sector involvement in peripheral rural and urban areas globally through infrastructure development in order to tackle unemployment, poverty, conflicts, rural-urban migration, linguistic diversity, and other sub-optimal outcomes.

Keywords: Connectedness, tajiriba spaces, sub-optimal outcomes, relatedness, urbanized neighborhoods

CHAPTER ONE

EXPLAINING SUB-OPTIMAL OUTCOMES

INTRODUCTION

Sub-optimal outcomes[1] are by definition either market failures, government failures or both. Imperfect market and/or government outcomes arise from the way society is structured along fault lines (relatedness) thereby making it difficult for the maximum utilization of human adaptive capacities.

THE FOUNDATION OF SUB-OPTIMAL OUTCOMES

Optimality represents the full utilization of all the resources (factors of production) available. This is when labour, capital[2], entrepreneurial capabilities, information, knowledge and natural resources (including land) are deployed to the best use possible. However, the structuring of the human society (relatedness) is such that it is not possible to fruitfully deploy all the available and potential resources.

---

[1] The idea of sub-optimal outcomes is associated with Vilfredo Pareto
[2] Capital is candidly monetized existing wealth

When people are excluded from the use of their adaptive capacity to meet their survival needs the consequences may manifest as adverse outcomes namely: unemployment, poverty, economic fluctuations, migration from rural to urban spaces, environmental destruction, resource wars, phenotypical stereotyping and identification and global terrorism.

With seven billion people living on planet Earth most of whom inhabit rural and far-flung locations, how to reduce run-away unemployment, poverty, rural-urban migration, identity struggles, global terrorism and other unsatisfactory outcomes in the world remain longstanding challenges.

The standard expectation is that the private sector should be able to deal with market efficiency challenges in the short, medium or long term. However, if the profit motive (individual/business interest) fails to correct sub-optimal allocation of resources then government intervention (public policy decisions) becomes inevitable.

Government policy interventions to correct market failure[3](s) may take the form of fiscal policy intervention (taxes),

---

[3] The first use of the phrase market failure is traced to Henry Sidgwick.

subsidies, bailouts, wage and price controls, regulations and direct provision of the good or service.

Government policy intervention measures must be guided by efficiency, effectiveness, equity, inclusiveness and sustainability considerations; otherwise government failure results.

Government failure may occur when public policy choices to correct market failure in turn result in inefficiencies in resource allocation.

Some scenarios dubbed 'relatedness dilemma[4]' may lead to both market failure and government failure. Relatedness dilemma is often caused by divisions in the human society (and the accompanying politics along these divisions).

Relatedness dilemma is a condition of inefficient allocation of value arising from thought processes, situations, circumstances and events that render state elites, illustrious academicians and private sector players' captive of politics of discrimination and competition.

For many years now, the state and private sector have attempted to deal with suboptimal outcomes without

---

[4] Relatedness dilemma refers to simultaneous market failure and government failure arising from politics along fault lines.

noteworthy success. The failure is largely because of the way the way human relations are structured.

Human identities stand in the way of sufficient mobility of labour, capital, information, people and knowledge. Competition, conflicts and wars represent improvident deployment of resources.

The world has an abundance of human and material resources. Unfortunately, these resources are misallocated, misapplied and underutilized. The misallocation, misapplication and underutilization of the vast natural human capacity and natural riches place the world society in a real dilemma.

Relatedness entrepreneurs (that include top state elites, politicians, distinguished academicians, captains of industry and average citizens) simply fuel divisions and competitions along fault lines. For politicians, human societal divisions are hunting ground for support and votes.

Whilst the state and private sector have been attempting to deal with market and government failures, the nonprofit sector has largely remained on the sidelines preoccupied with dealing with severe poverty, humanitarian and relief issues. However, it is now emerging that the partnership of the public sector, the private sector and the nonprofit sector can help restructure human relations to ensure fuller utilization of all human and material resources to engineer worldwide take-off.

The human population has grown in such size and complexity that it requires cooperation and collaboration in order to deploy all available (arable land, clean drinking water, precious metals, and fossil fuels) and potential resources (knowledge) to sustain the known universe.

To fully utilize world human and material resources it is important to collapse the boundaries that demarcate the human society into families, lineages, clans, castes, ethnicities, nation-states, races, religions and civilizations. Plainly put, an all-inclusive take-off can only happen with a mission-driven global integration.

Roughly speaking, there are two paradigms to global integration: globalization and connectedness.

Globalization thrives on schism, inequity, partition, injustice, vain rivalry and perilous face-offs while connectedness (global connectivity and togetherness) is inclusive, collaborative, forward-looking and value-laden.

Globalization grapples with a world defined by old animosities and differences, and therefore, promotes resource inefficiency. That being the case, globalization is underpinned by scarcity. According to globalization, earthly experiences (events and places) are explained by the struggle over the control of scant resources and mates. Nevertheless, the reality is that most of the universe is dominated by idle human capacity and huge tracts of transformable uninhabited locations.

Infinity (as opposed to scarcity and mortality) summarizes connectedness. Space is where events happen. Time is when events happen. Connectedness (infinity) ends the boundaries of time and space.

Connectedness is however more than just events and locations. Connectedness is about occurrences, places and destiny. It is about experiences, opportunities and possibilities. Succinctly put, connectedness is about spatial and non-spatial relations.

Holistically, the universe is constituted by physical location (matter/space/geography) and non-spatial relationships such as gravity, electromagnetism, strong nuclear interaction, weak nuclear interaction, dark matter, dark energy, mental faculties, senses, emotions, time, life and death (Khamala, 2015a). The universe is related as one unit in material and non-material realms.

Connectedness is a description of how apparently isolated features and occurrences evolve to form networks that is the universe as we know it.

Connectedness is premised on common hopes, mutual benefit and a shared goal (Khamala, 2014a; 2014b; 2014c; 2015a). The quest to sustain life weaves us together. We are connected and linked by experiences and possibilities.

Our increasing awareness of our connectedness is transforming the way we interact, communicate and strive desperately to cheat bereavement. As our adaptive capacities improve, the borderline that distinguishes between existence and bereavement increasingly becomes blurred.

For the most part of human history, instead of devoting our energies on safeguarding life and developing optimistic visions of the future premised on shared prosperity, we have constantly been plotting on how to outcompete or bring others down. Exploits of Alexander the Great, Napoleon and especially Adolf Hitler magnify the extent of our selfish appetite for glory and grandeur.

Today, global terrorists would wish the current human civilization to collapse without any better replacement. Civilizations collapse whenever they decay – they lose the focus to serve the will of the universe. The way to sustain our universal civilization is through continuous adaptation.

Technology (the capacity to manipulate our natural surroundings) offers humanity the opportunity to sustain or destroy life. The discovery of nuclear weapons signaled the perils of relatedness. It became too costly to continue business as usual. Connectedness enables us to handle big picture questions about humanity and its prospects.

Relatedness emphasizes scarcity of resources and income opportunities. It is however possible to restructure the world society along connectedness and to emphasize abundance of resources, income opportunities and possibilities.

Whereas relatedness limits the flow of resources, connectedness unleashes endless possibilities. Connectedness ensures that all surplus (underutilized) resources reach the international market.

Connectedness is about global (market) integration with the neighborhood acting as the fulcrum. The neighborhood stretches out worldwide analogous to a global village.

CONCLUSION

The market mechanism and state regulation determine value allocation in the human society. When markets are not working optimally government intervention may seek to correct for the distortions by improving the efficiency in markets operations. Sub-optimal outcomes arise in the event of market failures, government failures or a blend of both.

Because the human society is characterized by relatedness (e.g. globalization) it is prone to imperfections in the allocation of value. The price system and public sector regularly fail to bring about an equitable distribution of income and to utilize the world economy's resources fully.

Perfect allocation of value is synonymous with connectedness. This is when the human and material resources are fully engaged. Connectedness represents the adaptive face of capitalism.

CHAPTER TWO

TYPES OF SUB-OPTIMAL OUTCOMES

INTRODUCTION

Frequently, individuals and collectives desire to use their resources (adaptive capacities) to improve their individual and/or general well-being.

Resources include labour (ability to work), land, capital investments (buildings, equipment and other tools) and human capital[5] (the amount of competence and knowledge of how to combine factors of production to create useful products and services).

Every now and then, however, individuals and collectives end up using their resources in ways that don't advance their individual and/or general well-being.

Scientists scrutinize how society allocates its resources (adaptive capacities) among alternative uses and the consequences of these choices.

---

[5] Human capital refers to the stock of knowledge that can be used to produce something of economic value.

Sub-optimal outcomes represent inefficiencies in the allocation of resources (this may include misallocation, misuse, wastage and corruption).

The allocation of value in the world economy is characterized by inefficiencies contributing to suboptimal outcomes such as rural-urban migration; poverty and inequality; corruption; unemployment; identity struggles and wars; linguistic diversity and global terrorism.

RURAL-URBAN MIGRATION

Urbanization is a preferred outcome worldwide. It all began with the development of the earliest cities in Mesopotamia and Egypt.

Since the Enlightenment (Scientific Revolution, Industrial Revolution and Political Revolutions), the proportion of people that live in cities and their immediate surroundings has been increasing steadily over the years.

The recent phenomenal growth of towns and cities is because more and more people are leaving villages and farms to reside in urban areas and cities.

The United Nations projects most of the world population (75%) would live in urban areas by 2050 (UN HABITAT, 2007; UN, 2008).

Worldwide wealth is concentrated in privileged urban areas and big cities such that rural areas and slums don't have proper infrastructure, requisite amenities and social security.

Most income opportunities are also located in urban areas. The world's private sector is concentrated in cities and major towns. To avoid a life of misery, many people always flock to towns and cities in search of opportunities that are commensurate with their education and lifestyle.

Sadly, rural-urban migration exerts pressure on available resources. The inadvertent consequences of rural-urban migration include urban congestion; a rise in the number of the urban hungry, orphans and vulnerable children; pollution; unemployment; increased crime incidents; and the historical neglect of remote rural locations and urban slums.

Urban congestion means because people have to pay more for food, shelter, transportation and security. Pertinently, as most people gravitate towards cities, remote rural locations suffer an acute shortage of trained professionals and entrepreneurs.

Rural-urban migration is largely a no win situation. The world is rich in resources but because of the urban-rural divide, dusty villages lose out to major towns and cities. Unfortunately, the people moving to expanded towns and cities are more than the manageable levels.

Rural-urban migration trend can only be mitigated by taking development to the grassroots. It is more sustainable to alter the lives of rural dwellers gradually by urbanizing villages instead of the current situation characterized by rural-urban migration.

POVERTY AND INEQUALITY

Poverty is the deprivation of the capacity to utilize one's adaptive capacity to cater for basic human needs, which commonly include food, safe drinking water, sanitation facilities, clothing, shelter, health care, education and information.

Poor people are deprived of choices and opportunities. They cannot manipulate their environment for their own benefit requiring external intervention.

Roughly 1.2 billion people in the world live in a state of chronic poverty (UNDP Human Development Report, 2014).

Poverty is a major policy challenge. This is especially so given that world poverty is mostly in the rural and peri-urban areas. The unsavoury aspect of this skewed wealth distribution is that most of the people in rural areas living in poverty, feel voiceless and helpless in the debates that shape their lived experience.

Typically poor households can escape poverty by finding steady employment or through entrepreneurial activities. However, most of the world's poor lack income opportunities and access to even the most basic banking services, formal credit and insurance products which eventually holds back individuals and small businesses.

The microfinance credit programme pioneered by Muhammad Yunus of Grameen Bank only scratched the surface.

The universe is full of resources but because of the nexus between identities and scarcity, the abundance of resources (wealth) is often not accompanied by tangible benefits to the world population as a whole. For example, though the Democratic Republic of Congo is the richest country in Africa (with vast mineral resources), it has been plagued by a tragic history of abject poverty, atrocious exploitation, political conflicts and civil wars.

Poverty goes hand in hand with inequality. With most of the world wealth concentrated at the very top of the economic pyramid and in towns and cities inequality has become a huge challenge.

There is a screaming schism between the poor and the rich with almost half the world's wealth being owned by just 1 per cent of its population.

The wealth gap keeps on growing since inequality is built into the current growth model. This increased wealth disparity between the rich and poor drives a competitive society thereby risking social stability.

Inequality represents a major risk to evenhanded development in the longer term especially when so much income is concentrated in cities and towns.

High levels of inequality have a negative impact on both economic growth and poverty reduction. In the face of the mounting numbers of educated, unemployed and alienated graduates inequality stalls upward mobility. Unsurprisingly successive development plans and strategies on poverty reduction have not achieved much.

Neo-liberalism, the thinking behind globalization, suggests that the best medicine for global poverty and inequality are reforms to scale back the role of the state in the economy and to open sheltered markets to global investors.

Critics (Chomsky, 1999; Harvey, 2007; Duménil, 2013) observe that unchecked capitalism and the focus on growth-led policies prioritize the efficient utilization of capital rather the efficient use of resources. The end product is economic growth without development.

Thus far, trickle-down economics has failed to bring about greater justice and inclusiveness in the world. The growing inequality is due to emphasis on the absolute autonomy of the marketplace, financial speculation and the cutthroat competition in almost all spheres of life.

People all over the world recognize that the old way is not working for anyone. A sustainable model for poverty alleviation recognizes that experienced life is more than just material affluence and selfish pursuits.

Investing in people to tap their adaptive capacities represent the best way to forge social inclusion and reduce inequality over time. The creation of income opportunities is the pivotal link between economic growth and poverty reduction.

Implementing market-led economic policies alone may not guarantee advances and improvements in human well-being, prosperity and happiness. Poverty eradication calls for policies that focus on employment creation, productivity, social protection, and inclusion.

Achieving inclusive growth (reducing inequality) for disadvantaged people and locations requires the intervention of the non-profit sector to facilitate the adoption of policies that enable businesses to invest, grow, and create income opportunities.

The non-profit sector must be roped in to engage the market, attract investment, and create jobs. The aim is to ensure economic growth is distributed in a balanced manner to avoid extreme and excessive concentration of wealth and economic power

CORRUPTION

Graft is a global phenomenon, a universal challenge. The world is turning its back on exclusively state-led approach to economic development because of the corrupting tendencies associated with governments. The prevalent perception is that governments are not frugal in spending public funds.

Corruption and patronage occurs when individuals use public office for private gain. The end results include situations where politically-connected elites control most of a country's wealth and failure by governments to invest in health care, food security and essential infrastructure.

Some state officers also idle away in offices reading newspapers, gossiping, extracting rent by virtue of their office or impede the efficient operation of governmental machinery.

Corruption and patronage ensures that people with political connections control most of the world's wealth. Evidence abounds showing that concentrations of wealth and power distort democratic processes (Barbara, 2012).

Corruption skews priorities, destroys infrastructure, creates unequal society, multiplies grievances and generates tensions and conflicts.

Often, politically-connected thieving public officials collude to keep remote rural locations and urban slums in a state of permanent underdevelopment.

Because of corruption, competitive sourcing of employees (merit) is regularly in no way premised on potential valuable contribution to the common pool. Typically when people are employed without due consideration to qualification, experience, the capacity and/or willingness to do the work, opportunities for bias, discrimination and favoritism tend to arise. Surely, handing state jobs and tenders selectively and the subsequent separatist claims and allegations of neglect by the central government of named communities can prove dangerously divisive. This explains why it is wise to talk of marginalized places rather than marginalized communities.

Generally, corruption inhibits private investment, reduces economic growth, increases the cost of doing business and can lead to political instability.

Fighting sleaze is an arduous undertaking. Identities prevent the average (global) citizenry from holding government officials to account resulting in dismal delivery of public services. This has the risk of growing inequalities, increasing polarization and the world economy not operating at full potential.

Governments that are the products of identity struggles are frequently conservative and self-preserving. Such misguided regimes also take advantage of red tape, corruption and pilferage to engage in local, regional or global supremacy power struggles instead of improving governance, reforming their economies and making the world a better place for all.

Historically, governments that reward incompetence, laziness and corruption have failed miserably to attract and reward innovations, creativity and entrepreneurship.

Change starts at the margins and this is why scientific invention, innovation and entrepreneurship represent the major drivers of change around the world.

Change is only possible when hard work, thrift, diligent investments, diversification and industry attracts rewards.

The challenge of corruption is why the world is looking for nonprofit solutions for public problems.

UNEMPLOYMENT

Unemployment is a human crisis. Many governments worldwide are grappling with a major policy challenge of creating adequate, productive and sustainable jobs to absorb the growing labour force (ILO, 2014). Though many countries in the world have experienced exponential growth, huge populations of people remain unemployed and therefore poor.

Many people leave or graduate from schools, colleges and universities each year optimistic that they will find decent jobs or to start businesses in order to be economically independent. Regrettably, many of them, whether educated or not, are without work or an income.

There are no enough income opportunities to accommodate the ever-increasing number of school-leavers (and school drop-outs) that enter the labour market every year eager to apply the knowledge they have acquired and to participate in productive economic activities.

The failure to expand sufficiently fast to be able to make use of the readily available and willing human resources is commonly referred to as unemployment.

Conservative[6] estimates indicate that almost 202 million people around the world are unemployed. At current trends, global unemployment is set to hit 215 million job seekers by 2018 (ILO, 2014).

According to the ILO World Employment and Social Outlook Trends 2015 report, in 2014 unemployment stood at 201 million people. Global unemployment is expected to rise to 2012 by 2019. The European financial crisis helped shelve 61 million jobs. To close the global unemployment it is necessary to create 280 million jobs by 2019 (ILO, 2015).

The bulk of the increase in global unemployment is in low and middle income countries in Latin America and the Caribbean, China, the Russian Federation, the Middle East and Africa. The economy in low and middle income countries is largely informal.

The lack of opportunities for the unemployed to utilize their adaptive capacities has had some unintended, unforeseen and

---

[6] ILO (1982) considers the unemployed to be people who are out of work and are actively seeking for employment. This constricted definition overlook the population not economically active such as long-term unemployed who have despaired; the elderly; people with severe disabilities; those that are talented but lack academic qualifications (i.e. artists, musicians, poets, athletes, etc); homemakers; income recipients (i.e. rentiers); victims of redundancy; those in self-employment for lack of choice and the underemployed; persons engaged in community or volunteer work; and persons engaged in marginal activities. If this categories of people are considered then the number of those out of work could hit close to 1.5 billion people.

completely disastrous consequences. For starters, the unemployed are financially dependent on parents or guardians, friends and well-wishers.

Most of the unemployed are often pushed to indecent habitation, crime or even suicide. Others despair, become dejected or simply vegetate.

It is an open secret that millions of asylum seekers are fleeing from unemployment, idleness and other maladies that characterize our planet.

Most prohibited foreigners cannot work legally in their host countries and therefore barely survive.

On the whole, unemployment stagnates or shrinks the world economy. The general populace also suffers due to escalated rates of dependency, crime and conflicts, not forgetting to mention the opportunity costs of forced idleness.

Three major theoretical positions underpin the mitigation of unemployment: state intervention (Keynesianism and Socialism) and/or market mechanism (classical economics, neo-liberalism and Austrian economics). Either way, both supply-side solutions and demand-side solutions cannot achieve zero unemployment.

State intervention advocates robustly argue that the government has unique responsibilities that transcend commercial considerations. Governments provide for the public good while the private sector largely target to increase its profits. The government is obligated to stimulate the economy through public infrastructural projects.

Critics, however, observe that governments finance their activities, programmes and operations from taxes or borrowing (domestic or external). Expansion in public spending predominantly driven by recurrent expenditure pressures and mainly growth in public sector employees' emoluments poses the danger of crowding out the private sector from credit and slowing down the level of economic activities. Besides, pro-poor policies such as social assistance only work in the short term.

Impliedly creating job opportunities by increasing the public sector employee count is not a realistic alternative since the ballooning wage bill is a drain on public resources that would otherwise have been spent on development projects.

According to supply-side advocates the only meaningful way to resolve unemployment is through the expansion of the private sector. The private sector needs government to provide the legal systems, the basic security and the infrastructure to thrive.

Governments, on the other hand, rely on businesses to drive economic growth, create jobs and generate the much-needed foreign currency.

Expansion of public service wages inevitably lead to increase in deficit financing and inflation. Indeed, since the collapse of the Soviet Union and the ascendancy of globalization, most governments have been obsessed with keeping a low rate of inflation (single digit).

According to monetarism (the control of money supply), public sector jobs are rightfully considered recurrent expenditure, and as such, discouraged.

Of course, 'inflation-targeting' monetary policy to contain inflation has far-reaching implications on economic growth and employment. This explains why World Bank and IMF Structural Adjustment Programmes (SAPs) requirements to ensure debt obligations at the expense of economic transformation that is crucial to create jobs and reduce poverty are frequently strongly resisted.

SAPs of the 1990s led to massive restructuring of the Civil Service. Many civil servants were sent retrenched in order to reduce the wage bill and meet of the conditions for donor funding. Public service recruitment was halted. Many people were rendered redundant. Retrenchees relocated to their rural homes and slum areas to start a life of destitution and premature death.

SAPs sought to make the economies of emergent countries more market oriented. Increasing the scope of the private sector in the economies of developing countries must not necessarily lead to massive job losses. SAPs were a flop because they rendered many people without a stable source of income. These conditionalities were a threat to many people's livelihoods proving that reducing the number of civil servants by rendering some unemployed to rein the wage bill by right-sizing, restructuring, downsizing, retrenching or streamlining is effectively problematic.

Actually, attempts by countries to shrink their deficits (in the face of multiple currencies) through tax hikes and spending cuts hurt growth thereby complicating the unemployment crisis.

In the face of deficits, widespread wastage, corruption and red tape associated with government spending, the prevalent understanding is that job creation is the work of the private sector (individual initiative and enterprise). Then why isn't the private market guaranteeing meaningful employment opportunities?

The answer is relatively simple. Before a private investor opts to set up a business at a certain place the first consideration will be if the location is commercially viable. With a few exceptions, most secluded rural locations and slums are not business friendly. This explains why only a handful of locations especially in towns and cities are attracting the attention of private developers and investors.

The world cannot effectively manage sub-optimal outcomes unless infrastructural deficits and the accompanying income distribution are corrected. New policy approaches are required to attract enterprise in remote parts of the world and urban slums in order to expand income opportunities, raise household earnings, reduce poverty, and create a circle of investment and growth.

IDENTITY STRUGGLES, CONFLICTS AND WAR

Relatedness represents the great indelible divide, a growing cancer requiring an urgent solution. This is because identities are like minefields. They have the potential to eliminate the entire humanity when triggered.

Relatedness entrepreneurs use boundaries to gain political support. Exclusion politics (and the accompanying the triumphalist narrative) is the major causes of identity struggles, conflicts and war. Every year, millions of lives are lost, properties destroyed and families shattered worldwide because of identity differences.

Relatedness is responsible for the series of overlapping conflicts along multiple fault lines. Relatedness thrives and survives when the human society is demarcated. Choosing sides fuels and deepens the polarization, raises the possibility of violent encounters and even death.

Relatedness divides people and the human society into discrete competing and conflicting units. People conflict when they organize, scramble for the control of available resources or seek to expand under named label, attitudes and structures.

Hegemonic competition at any level of identification is a drag on economic growth, intellectual discourse and the search for practical solutions to problems afflicting society as it leads to less-than optimal resource utilization as manifest in unnecessary competition, skewed development and discrimination.

Genocide is the most perverse form of identity struggles. Genocide is the premeditated organized mass murder of people thought to be different to terminate their group existence.

Between 1975 and 1979, Pol Pot (born Saloth Sar) and many other loyalists of the Khmer Rouge (officially the Communist Party of Kampuchea) massacred nearly two million Cambodians during the failed stab to create a federation of collective farms (Kiernan, 1997).

Victims of the Cambodian genocide (mostly urban workers, soldiers, intelligentsia elites and ethnic minorities) died of deliberate starvation, overwork, lack of basic medication for treatable diseases, and frequently after being tortured or bludgeoned with clubs in a bid to save bullets. The underlying motivation for these horrid acts was the conviction in the superiority of the Khmer people, the predominant ethnic group in Cambodia.

Identity struggles and animosities were also responsible for the Holocaust, the Armenian genocide, the Kurdish genocide, Bosnian genocide, the Santa Cruz massacre in East Timor, the Guatemalan genocide, and the Rwanda genocide, among others.

The construction, fortification and endurance of identities have a gender dimension. Men and women play unequal roles in the construction, reinforcement and persistence of identities and in the relations between identities (Khamala, 2009).

Identities are constructed through gender inequality; reinforced through myths, symbols and rituals; and later manifest in a sophisticated power-play over resources, stature and supremacy.

And because change occurs at the margins, the gender equality movement is reshaping the nature, form and resolution of identities, identity struggles and identity conflicts.

The universe is overflowing with resources yet identity entrepreneurs compete for power, territory and mates along fault lines. This battle is happening worldwide.

Perennial competition among elites from rival identities has never been known to yield progress anywhere. In fact, clan, tribal, race, religious, gender or generation passion constrains the capacity for thought, reflection and action.

Fears of marginalization and attempts at domination often drive up social tensions and multiply conflicts. Successive politicians in the supposed bid to address the politics of marginalization and supremacy use perceived marginalization and superiority to their advantage for an easy ride to power. They promote a warped logic of recruiting the marginalized or the dominant and in turn ensure divisions along the margins remain intact, which further perpetuates the inefficient use of resources.

War is a global challenge that knows no boundaries. War is simply a struggle of warped values waged violently on local, regional or global scale involving states and/or non-state actors.

Majority of the people in the world do not like war situations since humans are born with a genetic inscription not to kill.

However, history is replete with examples of bureaucrats and politicians (relatedness kingpins) that turn ordinary people into murderous lunatics. Civil wars constitute the most predominant armed conflicts around the world.

In 1994, more than 800,000 people were butchered in Rwanda just because they belong to competing identities. Before the Rwanda massacre, different groups lived relatively peacefully together for much of the time and intermarriages were not uncommon. How can so many people be so gullible?

Often, narrow-minded political leaders manipulate identities for their own ends around election time thereby exacerbating tensions between mobilized social groups and the prospects for conflict. Educated and uneducated fools desecrate their adaptive capacity in maiming, killing, belittling, stereotyping, abusing and boasting of their superiority relative to others.

Many countries become failed states out of short-sighted policymaking. Relatedness often interferes with the commencement and implementation of inclusive alternative policy platforms. The basic facts are very clear, without relatedness world militaries are simply a waste. The ethnic origin of modern states explains why (nation-) states can be predatory.

Historically states have annexed other states premised on popular will, historic grievance, divine providence, ethnic reunification (e.g. Sudetenland) and even dream of world conquest.

Indonesia invaded East Timor in 1975. Morocco absorbed Western Sahara in 1975. Saddam Hussein in 1990 attempted to make Kuwait the nineteenth province of Iraq. India and Pakistan have fought three wars since independence from Britain in 1947.

In 2013, mainly Muslim Seleka rebels seized power in Central African Republic (CAR) perpetrating abuses on the majority Christian population that triggered waves of revenge attacks by anti-balaka militias on Muslims leading to thousands of displacements and deaths.

In March 2014, more than twenty years after the disintegration of the former Soviet Union, Vladimir Putin invaded Ukraine and proclaimed Crimea as part of Russian territory allegedly to protect ethnic Russians.

In recent times, Japan, Indonesia, Singapore, Vietnam, the Philippines, Brunei, Taiwan and Malaysia have made competing territorial claims over resource-rich waters of the

South China Sea. Canada, Russia and Denmark are separately contending to grab the North Pole.

Finally, most conspicuously is the long-simmering tensions and vicious fighting between the Sunni, Shiite (and sometimes Kurdish) Muslim sects.

Geopolitics is obviously discomforting. The collapse or dissolution of the Soviet Union (then a powerful empire with global influence and ideological appeal) was for Putin "the greatest geopolitical catastrophe" of the 20th century. The old Cold War mentality still reigns supreme (Foreign Affairs, May/June 2014: 69-79). Putin is convinced of the existence of a conspiracy to surround Russia with hostile neighbors.

The Ukrainian crisis has its roots in Putin's desire to build a post-Soviet economic zone (Eurasian Economic Union) comprising many former Soviet republics including Russia, Belarus, Armenia, Kazakhstan and Kyrgyzstan. Russian reunification targets to re-establish Russian regional dominance against the 28-menber-state European Union. Friendly Ukraine is vital to Russia's defense. The same can be said of the Baltic States. Russia has been forced to rely on proxies and nuclear deterrence.

Therefore, the geopolitics of the Black Sea, the Caribbean and the South China Sea, among others mirrors the Darwinian struggle for survival commonly associated with relatedness.

But this logic has run its course.

We have to do things differently. Thoughtless competition and military intervention along historical, geographical, religious, racial and or ethnic ties do not surmise anymore. According to connectedness, geopolitics should be about economic, political and social ties to the world.

Morals are not relative. Wars happen because people mistakenly suppose that the universe lacks a common value system and goal. However, connectedness thinking suggests that an individual's welfare and fate is tied to that of others. Accordingly, contests and bloodbath along and among identities inhibits the human capacity to explore, tame and manipulate their immediate and remote locale.

To prevent war in the state system the grassroots must shape the choice of leaders and leadership. People who are rewarded with public office for successfully violently persecuting grievances along fault lines almost always never change tact. Such leaders perpetuate an atmosphere of continuous crisis and grievance to maintain support and relevance.

However, identity struggles and the accompanying conflicts and wars only benefit the hawks and cartels of national elites especially those in the weaponry and ammunition industry. Often, small and medium sized businesses are forced to close shop and their owners are forced to enroll in the armies. Tensions and fault lines assist hawks to win office as compared with doves.

A wind of change is sweeping across the world. Soon there may possibly be no 'borders' separating countries. The improvement in transport is facilitating integration places, improving market access, and encouraging spatial agglomeration. The Internet and social networks are opening up borders and collapsing boundaries by connecting people. A lot of effort is being expended to bring Internet connectivity to more remote areas using drones and satellites.

It is unimaginable that instead of networking and consummating emotions people would take up arms to fight unreasonable wars. Worse to imagine entrepreneurs closing shop to join the war machine then to start all over again at a loss (unemployed) after war ends.

Given our connectedness, Putin's foray in Crimea under the old-fashioned pretext of protecting Russian speakers is a major drawback. The same can be said of territorial disputes over the South China Sea.

The efficacy of the use of military force by (nation-) states has all along been overrated. In retrospect, today the state is about location. The state is a spatial entity. No wonder military dominance is fading as the tide of war recedes. The civilized state is not an end in itself. The state works at the behest of individual(s) to sustain life.

ECONOMIC FLUCTUATIONS

The invention of money ranks as one of the peak discoveries by humankind. Money is an incentive/pricing mechanism. Money oils the market economy. It drives relationships, discoveries, innovations, inventions and enterprise. Without such a mechanism the invisible hand of the market falters. This is because individuals respond to incentives. Almost all socialist experiments have failed demonstrating that without incentives people put in the bare minimum.

The world payment and settlement system is characterized by multiple currencies as informed by competing (state) identities. Identities interfere with the world currency market's capacity to self-organize.

One of the costs the world pays for erecting and maintaining identities (multiple currencies) is economic fluctuations. Economic fluctuations are principally the product of speculative capital flows.

Economic fluctuations are a permanent fixture of the world economy just like the way identity struggles fluctuate so do currencies. The multiple currency system is meant to satisfy our ego. However, the bitter truth is that today dollarization[7] is the trend rather than the exception.

The US dollar is the world reserve currency (giving America the latitude to pay its bills by printing money, incurring debts and/or raising taxes to shore up outsized government budget deficits and to maintain a worldscale military establishment).

Foreign imports and transactions by majority of the countries are as a rule procured in US dollars. Having many national payment and settlement platforms mostly facilitate speculation (deflation and inflation) and of course unemployment.

---

[7] Dollarization refers to the use of parallel currencies, shared currencies and/or currency unions

For Keynesians, the government needs to spend more to generate better outcomes. On the contrary, monetarists believe that government spending crowds out private sector from credit and investment. The more the Government borrows the fewer the funds available for the private sector to borrow. Austrians believe that the government is bad and needs to be reduced or eliminated altogether.

Inefficiency, misallocation or issuing too much money contributes to high inflation or even hyperinflations as a result of too much money chasing too few goods reflecting the world's deeply intertwined economic relations.

Currency debasement occurs when the local currency diminishes its value in the global currency market and results in lower living standards.

When the import bill is still higher than what is received from exports, borrowing externally could expose the local economy to adverse exchange rate risk. The bulk of the ballooning foreign debt service obligations arise because of multiple currencies. Foreign denominated debt, direct aid and other budgetary support measures effectively means ceding of monetary sovereignty.

Economic fluctuations arise because the world lacks a comprehensible roadmap. Globalization thrives on multiple currencies. Given that inflation and unemployment are polar opposites, no country on its own can achieve zero unemployment. This also implies that unless interventions are made rural and far-flung regions may remain underdeveloped for a long time.

LINGUISTIC DIVERSITY AND MULTILINGUALISM

The world's 7 billion people probably speak between 5,000 and 7,000 different languages. Knowing the exact number of human languages in the world is delicate since there are no clear boundaries between a language and a dialect. Linguistic diversity broadly refers to the existence of the array of important dissimilarities displayed by human languages.

The most common languages in terms of number of speakers are Mandarin Chinese, Spanish, English, Bengali, Hindi, Portuguese, Russian, Japanese, German, Wu Chinese and Arabic. English is the most important language of wider communication in the world. English is also the main language of science and technology.

Linguists theorize that the future is multilingual. Multilingualism, the capacity to use more than one language in a speech community, is now a common phenomenon. The prevalence of multilingualism arises from imperialism (i.e. slavery, colonialism, neo-colonialism, globalization, etc.); migration, relocation and resettlement movements; increased contact among different parts of the world; safeguarding of disappearing languages; education (the embracing of second and foreign languages); and religious movements.

Languages have been disappearing and becoming extinct. A language disappears when it is no longer transmitted to the next generation.

The politics of language diversity arise from the fact that each language has its native (first) speakers. People become worried when the number of people with the ability to speak or understand their mother tongue is in the minority. Desperate attempts are being made the worldwide to 'save' endangered language varieties. The measures include the teaching of vernacular in lower primary.

Language politics[8] can also take the form of the existence or absence of preferential treatment of one or several language(s)

---

[8] How linguistic diversity is managed in the political arena.

over another and/or other languages. For example, the Sharpeville massacre in Soweto in 1976 happened because school children were resisting attempts to force them to learn Afrikaans as a basic requirement if they were to advance in education.

The future is not multilingual. Actually, the future is monolingual; characterized by linguistic homogeneity. True, the number of languages (spoken and written) is diminishing drastically. Nevertheless, propping languages that are on the verge of extinction is unnecessary. Language is the bridge for connectedness. Even multilingualism is simply a transitory phase towards perfect linguistic homogeneity.

GLOBAL TERRORISM

Terrorism is a set of violent practices undertaken by non-state actors against civilian populations and state agents to achieve political ends. Terrorism is often used to spread negative emotions (i.e. fear, grief, despair, etc.) and targets to achieve ends that could not otherwise be achieved by peaceful and legal means.

Global terrorism is fuelled in part by dissatisfaction with the dividends of shared universal worldviews. Global terrorists are not motivated by self-gain but devastation.

Globalization, the current leading thought model, encourages radicalized groups to thrive largely driven by perceptions of being on the periphery. Such understanding may help explain the rise of Osama bin Laden's Al-Qaeda; the Taliban of Afghanistan and Pakistan; Boko Haram of Nigeria; Al-Shabaab of Somalia and the Islamic State in Iraq and Syria.

All in all, global terrorism is a travesty since fanaticism, extremism and intolerance only breeds cycles of violence, marginalization and disadvantage. There are more reasonable, effective and humane means to persecute grievances (e.g. peaceful protests, marches and provision of income opportunities) without resorting to terror tactics that often invoke thoughtless brutality.

Human engagement is not merely about identities engaging in fierce competition for nature's resources and power. The universe gyrates around geography, demographics, experience and providence (the possibility of immortality).

Life and death are opposites and as such coheres. Happy people are content with living (endlessly). Unhappy people are disconnected with life (as they know it). They are frustrated and alienated from the mainstream society. For them, experienced life is not worthy living. They prefer another life (unknown life). War, terrorism and suicidal attacks are demonstrations of disconnectedness.

The world is certainly not an unfair place. However, less-than-adequate outcomes such as unemployment, poverty, inequality, identity struggles, conflicts, wars make people lose their connection with the universe. Dissatisfied people can be driven into dastardly crime and spurious enterprises. Terrorism is an extreme form of disconnectedness.

Disconnectedness revolves around negative emotions such as fear, anger, disgust, jealousy, sorrow, sadness, envy, quilt and hatred. The emphasis is on enmity, fear, self-interest, self-sacrifice or simply despondency.

Disconnectedness often has negative effects on mental health; and is the greatest risk factor for suicide, homicide and even mass murder.

Terrorists, separated from normal life by an ocean of hostility and fright, unleash indiscriminate violence so that ordinary people live in fear of arbitrary things that can happen to them.

We are witnessing an emerging new worldview. With the ascendancy of connectedness and the subsequent decline of relatedness, the influence of violence and war in human affairs is going to wane.

Connectedness revolves around feelings of positive emotions such as happiness, care, appreciation, joy, love, empathy, sympathy, compassion. The emphasis is on friendship, collaboration, social networks or simply happiness. While happiness remains subjective, it has a beneficial effect on our own health and well-being, and can have a positive effect on those around us.

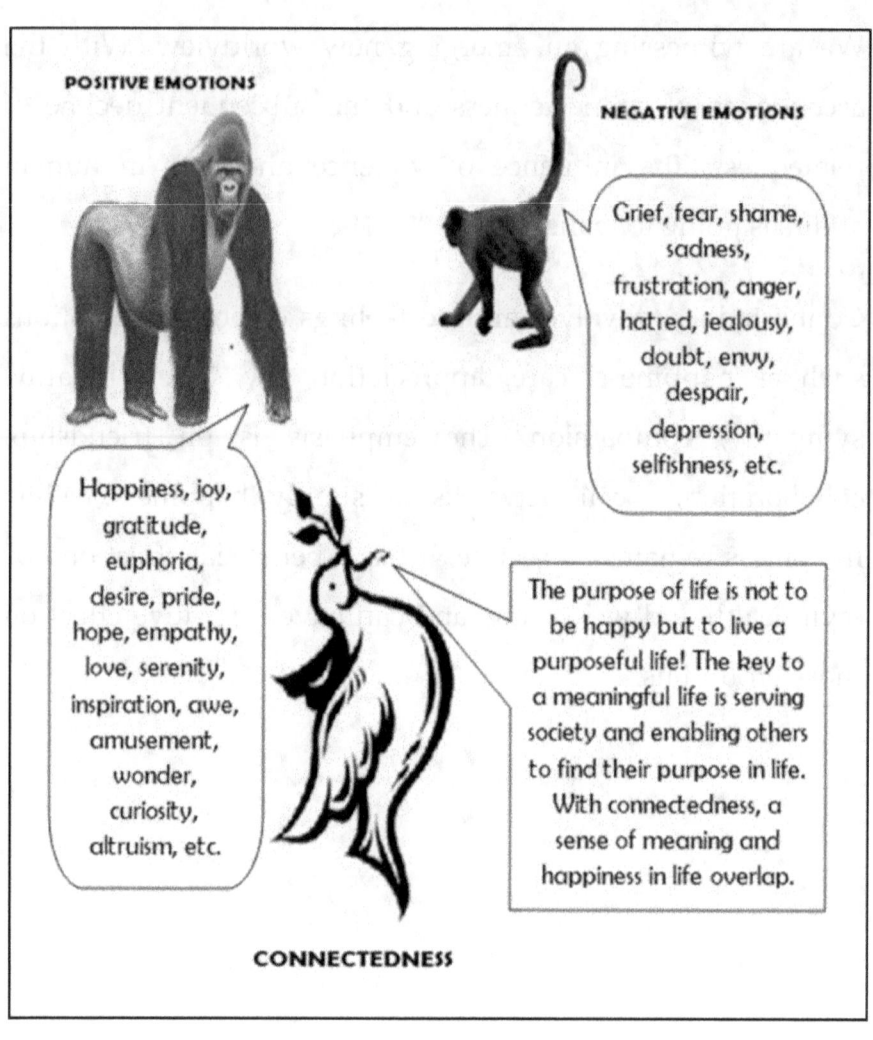

Fig. The Meaning of Life

In 1785, James Hutton (1726 - 1797) originated the idea of approaching the world holistically with reference to the history, age and structures of the Earth's crust. Today, evidence abounds demonstrating that what happens on one side of the world affects the other.

Nature never dictates our choices in life. Instead nature often plays games with us by giving us choices to a predetermined end. Whichever choice we make we end up with the same result – life preservation. The universe is precisely tailor-made for the emergence and sustenance of life. Unfortunately, the choices we make dictate our experience.

CONCLUSION

People as individuals and collectives desire to deploy their adaptive capacities (resources) to survive and thrive. However, relatedness (the current structuring of the world society) renders the allocation of value problematical. That being the case, the world is characterized by suboptimal outcomes namely rural-urban migration; poverty and inequality; corruption; unemployment; identity struggles; and global terrorism.

CHAPTER THREE

REMEDIES FOR SUB-OPTIMAL OUTCOMES

INTRODUCTION

Scientists consider the consequences of allocative decisions in order to redress non-ideal outcomes. Some of the approaches suggested to generate more desirable outcomes include Classical Economics; Marxism, neo-Marxism and post-Marxism; Keynesianism and post-Keynesianism; Austrian Economics; Monetarism (Chicago School of Economics); and Neo-Liberalism (The Washington Consensus), among others.

This write-up demonstrates that the better approach is one that embraces connectedness.

Connectedness blurs the divide between developed and developing countries; blends together private, public and non-profit sectors; devalues the rural-urban continuum; embraces mixed development; envisages borderless borders in order to facilitate the free movement of goods, services and people worldwide; and promotes neighborhood diplomacy.

Connectedness can be achieved through a worldwide network of neighborhoods - Tajiriba Spaces[9]. Tajiriba Spaces are

48

locations anywhere in the world for facilitating the optimal application of human adaptive capacities.

Connectedness places a high premium on value systems that appreciate the meaningfulness of human interaction and social contact. In a connectedness world, leading a meaningful life is the ultimate goal.

URBANIZED NEIGHBOURHOODS

Historically, the urge to belong (relatedness) has taken precedence over other mechanisms of securing human life. However, segregation is now becoming a thing of the past. Connectedness (integration) treats humanity as a unified whole.

Urbanized neighborhoods (hamlets, villages and slums) have the potential to boost connectedness worldwide thereby redress the lingering identity struggles. A successful neighborhood is one where nobody is excluded from productive activities and the allocation of value.

Preferably each village/urban slum should have a Tajiriba Space to act as the face of that particular neighborhood. The

---

[9] Tajiriba Spaces are urban settings in remote rural areas and urban slums

point is to stimulate the penetration of individual and private enterprise and create new markets in places where without such intervention there isn't sufficient effective demand to justify investments.

Tajiriba Spaces are attempts to stimulate additional income opportunities (thereby make the sharing of world resources possible) by prioritizing infrastructural expansion as a strategy of devolving progress to isolated rural areas and urban slums.

Through Tajiriba Spaces, it is possible to urbanize villages (and develop slums) in so doing create billions of new income opportunities to fully utilize human adaptive capacities, improve infrastructure and spur the world economy.

More than half of humanity already lives in major towns and cities (UN HABITAT, 2007; UN, 2008). The current mode of urbanization takes the form of rural-urban migration which is unsustainable in the short-term and in the long run.

Tajiriba Spaces are mechanisms to achieve sustainable urbanization. Urbanizing hamlets, villages and slums can heal demarcations in the human society thereby help the world to deal with below par outcomes.

TRANSFORMING DEMARCATIONS

The world is organized along fault lines (relatedness). Demarcations in the human society are essentially about perception (with the twin ideas of life and death as the organizing principle).

The first demarcation is premised on levels of development.

The world is divided on the basis of development status into the haves (developed/global south/first world) and the have-not (developing/global south/third world). There is also the second world, the fourth world and peripheral development. Tajiriba Spaces are meant to facilitate neighborhoods (village-to-village) relationships to blur the divisions among the 196 countries in the world on the basis of common hopes, mutual benefit and shared values.

The second demarcation is based on national currencies. Traditionally, each country has had its own domestic currency. Domestic currencies are a source of great pride for citizens. Many believe that adopting a foreign currency symbolizes foreign control (enslavement to an alien monetary policy). Recently, however, the world is witnessing increasing dollarization in the face of the perils of economic fluctuations.

The world requires a grander coalescing vision to manage or purge economic fluctuations. Connectedness envisions a universal currency. In the meantime, the consequences of economic fluctuations can be dealt with through a global network of neighborhoods. Through Tajiriba Spaces, it is possible to sustain global growth and avoid stagnation or collapse that commonly arises in a world characterized by multiple currencies.

The third demarcation is based on the profit motive. Good and services are essentially offered by the profit sector, public sector and/or non-profit sectors. Neo-Liberalism (globalization), the dominant thinking, privileges private enterprise. Connectedness merges the three sectors to optimally serve a higher purpose.

Tajiriba Spaces are free and open pool of resources to benefit the world through the facilitation of enterprise, human creativity and benevolence. Tajiriba Spaces are motivated by the human impulse to make a difference in the lives of others; to serve a greater good. Nobody can own Tajiriba Spaces.

There is also the distinction between a hamlet[10], village, town and city. Historically, we have had rural spaces (hamlets and villages) and urban spaces (towns and cities) based on the concentration of people. The number, size and location of human settlements determined whether a location was to be categorized a group of houses (a hamlet), village, town or city. It is suggested that hamlets and villages are inhabited by a few hundred residents while urban systems are associated with thousands or even millions of residents.

Connectedness contends the rural-urban continuum on the understanding that urban life is not defined by mazes of concrete and steel. Neither is it defined by concentrated, dense populations. Indeed, nowadays most hamlets and villages are sizably populated. The bottom line is that what defines urban life is inclusivity in the allocation of value. Hamlets, villages and urban slums are characteristically exclusive in the application of resources. Looking ahead, Tajiriba Spaces will render the designation of a hamlet, village, town and city moribund.

The fourth demarcation is one based on infrastructure. Infrastructure (especially transport and enterprise infrastructure) plays a decisive role in resource allocation and

---

[10] A hamlet is a small village often made up of a group of homesteads

use. Urban places are outstandingly characterized by first-rate infrastructure while rural spaces and slums stand out for the deficit of appropriate infrastructure.

Tajiriba Spaces are mechanisms for financing shared infrastructural projects. The expectation is that as people find urbanized neighbourhoods attractive, they will come with their labour, purchasing power and tax revenues. Over time, as effective demand and the tax base increase, so will the infrastructure, goods and social services.

In the past, it was important to categorize goods and services into low-order, medium order and high-order as theorized by Walter Christaller[11].

Low order goods are time-to-time products and services, small in value, frequently purchased, and are inexpensive. Low-order goods include food (i.e. milk, bread, sweets and grocery items) and other routine household items and appliances. Middle-order products are items and services that are bought on a regular basis but not as frequently and cheap as low-order products and services. High-order products are basically luxury items. They are costly, have a limited market and are hardly replenished.

---

[11] Walter Christaller formulated Central place theory

In recent years, there have been many drastic changes in shopping patterns; how people shop and where they shop. Many people now prefer to shop at one-stop superstores where they can buy all they need in one place. Goods and services which were considered expensive and bought less often are now considered routine purchases.

Because all goods and services are in high demand, people prefer to buy them to be offered in close proximity. As such, people don't have to plan to go to major towns and cities to shop for specialized and high value everyday items. Looking ahead, Tajiriba Spaces will primarily provide almost all goods and services to its adjacent population.

The change in the way people shop (and shopping locations) is blurring the classification of goods and services into low-order, middle order and high-order. The distinction will blur further with the establishment of Tajiriba Spaces and the accompanying steady flow of customers. Tajiriba Spaces represent one-stop centres for convenient shopping experience in remote rural places and slums.

Related to the change in shopping patterns is the ongoing abandonment of zoning. Traditional zoning that segregated land uses into residential, commercial, industrial and agricultural is giving way to mixed-use development and walkable neighborhoods. Tajiriba Spaces are in sync with mixed development.

The seventh demarcation is based on lifestyle. Traditionally, we had slum lifestyle, rural lifestyle, and urban or city lifestyle. Through Tajiriba Spaces, it is possible to upgrade rural and slum lifestyles. The logic is to support physical infrastructure development and guarantee income opportunities in remote locations and urban slums to unleash inclusive growth.

Finally, urbanized neighborhoods may change our perception of home. Home is where you prosper (Aristophanes[12], n.d.). Home is where you flourish. However, prosperity is meaningless if it does not help society to fulfill its goals.

Home is not merely any habitual dwelling place. Home is where you discover the meaning of your life and possibly help others to discern the purpose and meaning of their existence. People need meaning to prosper. The purpose and meaning of life is to advance the will of the universe.

---

[12] Aristophanes (448 – 380 BCE) said, "A man's homeland is wherever he prospers".

Home can mean the place where one lives permanently or otherwise. However, no one is ever free from the influence of their environment (experience). This conceptualization is in line with connectedness which blends the material realm and immaterial realm. Home is, therefore, a place plus the accompanying experience (memories, feelings of attachment and other emotions) in the struggle to maintain life.

Home is not a fixed place but is mediated by new places, people and experiences and the sense of belonging. Home can be any location anywhere in the world. And, it is possible to have more than one home. However, our childhood home(s) (the place(s) where we were born and grew up) is the most memorable and often linger on in all our lives.

Historically, perceptions of home have been consistently colored by reference to the place where a person was born (and raised). Understood this way, the concept home from time to time refers to natives or indigenous inhabitants (and in some cases those closely related by birth) especially as distinguished from those not born in a particular place (i.e. nonnative population, outsiders, strangers, foreigners, etc.).

Subsequently, persons born (or that grew) in another area than that lived in are perceived or treated differently inducing a sense of alienation and detachment. Persons belonging to a place since birth or childhood feel a sense of loss for hosting 'recent intruders'.

Tajiriba Spaces blurs the boundary between the place one happens to live and the place one thinks of as home. Urbanized neighborhoods offer people the opportunity to belong, define their individuality and realize a sense of purpose through the full utilization of their adaptive capacities to achieve collective human goals regardless of location and/or place of birth.

Experiences in urbanized locations are meant to rekindle our childhood memories and feelings, make better our life experiences and inspire our hopes for the future. That being the case, home can be whichever location everyplace in the world. It is possible to have many homes (memorable experiences).

The bottom line is that urbanized neighborhoods hold the key to realizing the best possible outcomes. To promote holistic progress, every neighborhood must aspire to transform itself into a net importer of knowledge, skills and expertise by attracting additional residents and a net exporter of goods, services and goodwill. The net result would be more income opportunities, improved infrastructure, better access to quality goods and social services, and threefold increase in tax revenues.

Tajiriba places revolve around the non-profit sector and are cushioned from the profit motive, politics and government interference.

They should be able to operate professionally like businesses with strong emphasis on meticulous planning, foresight, efficiency, effectiveness but with a humanitarian bend. Recruitment of managers should be based on ability, commitment and potential to achieve regardless of other considerations. The ablest and best-qualified individual with the greatest potential should be given the opportunity to serve.

The expectation is that Tajiriba Spaces will opportunely give investors, entrepreneurs, shoppers, interns, workers and donors the prospect to invest, shop, live, work and support any neighborhood anywhere in the world in an attempt to build a cohesive wider society.

Indeed, while it is not prudent or even feasible to stop people from migrating from remote rural locations, it is possible to retain a good section of the populace and even attract more others from elsewhere by making these locations attractive to investments.

CONCLUSION

Despite all the development, the world is still home to plenty of untamed hinterland and unused human capacity. Investing in infrastructure is the single most effective means of reducing poverty, managing unemployment and staving rural-urban migration among other adverse effects.

Tajiriba Spaces are potentially the most transformative arenas to realize favourable outcomes worldwide premised on common hopes, mutual benefit and a shared goal thereby connecting every single person and neighborhood to the rest of the world.

CHAPTER FOUR

BENEFITS OF TAJIRIBA SPACES

INTRODUCTION

World over, infrastructure is critical for start-ups and the growth and expansion of existing business.

Discouragingly, in many parts of the world, urban environments are associated with mega infrastructure projects while rural spaces and slums are without even the most basic infrastructure.

Subsequently, the expansion of enterprise in rural and slum environments has largely been constrained by poor transport network and the lack of suitable property facilities to lease. To complicate matters lately governments faced with increasing financing pressure for both growth and recurrent expenditure are turning to alternative sources of finances to carry out infrastructural projects.

No individual or entity can solve the challenges of less-than-optimal resource utilization on its own. Through Tajiriba Spaces it is possible to bring together a variety of players to address this challenge collectively. Tajiriba Spaces are urbanized neighborhoods in remote rural locations and slums that have upgraded the application of human adaptive capacities.

Urbanizing neighborhoods is the best collective incentive to help the world community to cultivate and achieve collective goals premised on a collective value system. Tajiriba Spaces exemplify a public good provided by the non-profit sector for the benefit of the whole society.

Policywise, Tajiriba Spaces represent a smart approach to capturing the resulting value from public investments for the whole society. The role of governments may be limited to goodwill, the enabling legislation and, where necessary, tax breaks, incentives and subsidies.

This considered approach represents a sea-change for policy in a bid to seal the huge gap between public investments needs and available resources.

Tajiriba Spaces are economically necessary to enhance the world economy, deal with inequality among many other benefits.

The numerous advantages that can be associated with Tajiriba sites and locations are discussed in detail below.

SUSTAINABLE CONNECTEDNESS

Ever since the dawn of civilization people have pondered over wherefores of identity – the structuring of the universe and human society. For many years, people have used creation and migration myths, symbols and rituals to explain the basis, benefits, drawbacks and endurance of distinct identities. Using models, observation, experiments and everyday sensations, scientists have grappled to interpret the codification of nature and the place of identities in the scheme of things.

However, in the fullness of time the origin and future of identities (or polarity) remains unsatisfactorily answered. Today, identities manifests in the human society as families, lineages, clans, castes, ethnicities, nation-states, races, religions and civilizations.

As for the purpose of identities, this is a subject of much discussion and debate. According to connectedness, identities trace their origin in their usefulness as a mechanism to protect life (endlessly where possible) (Khamala, 2014a; 2014b; 2014c).

The incest taboo, which is almost universal and that has a biological basis, besides preventing the health setbacks associated with inbreeding, it also helps to avoid competition and conflict that may lead to premature death within the family.

The survival of the family and current social organization and patterns rests on the restriction of sex among its members and the consequent need for other family units as sources of spouses. The incest taboo normally extends to close (and sometimes distant) relatives for the same purpose thus bringing into its fold lineages and exogamic clans.

The family unit and the consecutive socio-political identities arising thereof cushion members from early death. Fatefully, relatedness is a double-edged sword. These socio-political and economic institutions simply solidify human groups, redirect and externalize competition, conflict and death. Patently, almost all adverse outcomes correlate with botched attempts to establish, maintain or dismantle asymmetrical power relations (or hegemonies).

Relatedness and connectedness determine human behavior and relations in society. Both relatedness and connectedness deal with society and relationships among individuals within the society.

Relatedness has always been central to people's lives. The human society has often been divided into separate kinship groups. Inadvertently, identities have long been characterized by long-running feuds, historical grievances and bloody encounters. The reasons are obvious.

From a policy perspective, connectedness offers an alternative way of organizing society instead of human restricted enclaves based on relatedness. Sustainable connectedness is anchored on a clear demonstrable common goal or value system.

Connectedness permeates our view of relationships and interactions with the environment. Against this backdrop, sub-optimal outcomes are therefore self-inflicted challenges.

The great cities of Jericho, Uruk, Mari, Memphis, Ur, Yinxu, Thebes, Babylon, Carthage, Alexandria, Rome, Constantinople, Baghdad, Kaifeng, Damascus and Cairo withered and collapsed because they were demonstrably premised on relatedness.

The Hadrian's Wall and the Great Wall of China are historical reminders of the pitfalls of relatedness as a basis for organizing the world society.

The Roman Emperor Hadrian who reigned from 117 to 138 CE built the impressive 80 miles long Hadrian's Wall to separate the Romans from the barbarians. Hadrian's Wall mirrored Rome's power and might. However, relatedness (boundaries) has never been a sustainable basis for organizing human relationships. On August 24, 410 CE the Germanic tribes successfully invaded and ransacked Imperial Rome.

The Great Wall of China was originally conceived by Emperor Qin Shi Huang (259-210 BCE) to fortify the Chinese Empire from incursions by barbarian warlike nomads and the influence of foreign ideas (Li & Zheng, 2001). These walls, fortresses and fortifications never effectively prevented invaders and plunderers from entering China. Indeed, China was ultimately successfully invaded, ravaged and pillaged by Genghis Kan Mongol troops. Paradoxically, the Great Wall contributed to the isolation of China from the rest of the world.

The progress of time has demonstrated the futility of building walls, fortresses, fencing, watch towers, night-vision cameras and radar.

Sustainable connectedness necessitates beneficial contact, knowledge sharing and shared perspectives. Material advancements and technological innovations proceed rapidly in societies that are intimately connected with outside societies. Isolated geographical locations often lag behind.

Urban settings are mostly a boon to human interaction, exchange and more opportunities for people to progress. Urban systems can grow sustainably and shape a new global framework premised on connectedness. Connectedness is a new model of partnership based on shared values and interests, mutual respect and common aspirations.

Power has its perils. History is awash with people who were victims of the perils of latitude and affluence. Politics is not necessarily is a zero sum game. However, until we settle the issue of identity, identity struggles will continue limiting our ability to explore and tame the universe. It is the cost of identity politics that has forced us to confine ourselves to short-termism and minimalist thinking.

In this day and age, we can no longer delude ourselves that the four factors of production, that is, land, labour capital and information, are scarce. What is lacking is the awareness that we are governed by a common goal and value system.

International relations revolve around diplomacy (life) and war (death). People who are in tune with their environment prefer diplomacy over war.

Diplomacy revolves around inclusiveness (connectedness). Relatedness, which manifest as polarity, globalization, war and other forms of competition is a sign of disconnectedness.

Majority of wars are caused by the pursuit of power and territorial claims. Wars centers negative emotions such as self-interest, isolation, competition and win-lose scenarios. However, the world is gradually breaking away from the historical pattern of conflicts and confrontation preferring compromise, cooperation and mutual benefit.

Pundits and policymakers have been trying to find truly sustainable and global solutions to improve the state of the world. The standard expectation has been that private and governmental entities should lead the way in solving sub-optimal outcomes due to the public and private resources at their disposal.

Today, the landscape is changing dramatically on the realization that governments and the private sector alone can't solve unemployment, infrastructural deficits and other sub-optimal outcomes. A new global multi-stakeholder community has to emerge at the borderlands to drive sustainable development.

Strategically speaking, sustainable connectedness is about improving infrastructure, lifting trade barriers and opening corridors to facilitate trade, exchange and interaction on a word scale. This is a process that started many years ago.

The human ability to precisely communicate abstract and learned information allowed humans to discover religion, tools, fire, agriculture, animal husbandry, the Internet and the spread of mobile telephony, including mobile banking. Other significant processes include the discovery of money, the surfacing of the modern state and the materialization of legal frameworks (constitutions).

Peaceful instruments for facilitating peaceful relations on the world scale include conciliation, mediation, negotiation, compensation, arbitration, adjudication, enforcement of awards, treaties, the formation of international organizations like the UN, etc.

The non-profit sector can shape and influence global integration. Instead of a struggle of conflicting values waged on a global scale the emphasis can be on unity of efforts that transcends (state) boundaries.

The non-profit sector has pioneered the best mechanisms for rewarding hard work, thrift, innovation and philanthropy.

Think of the Nobel Prizes, the Oscars, just to a mention the most exemplary.

The nonprofit sector is also behind efforts to foster accountability, good governance, development and the mitigation against conflicts. Non-profits like the Ford Foundation, Human Rights Watch, the Aga Khan Development Network (AKDN), churches, synagogues, temples and mosques have strongly supported diverse political, economic and social transformations.

The Internet Corporation for Assigned Names and Numbers (ICANN), a not-for-profit organization, secures the global internet security from 1997. ICANN has struggled to have a freehand in the management of the Internet domain name system without interference from state and non-state actors. ICANN is transforming itself from an institution overseen by the US government into a globally representative body. The transition to a more international institution that coordinates unique names for websites is in line with increased global connectedness.

Historically, the human awareness of our connectedness and the consequent capacity to transform nature (technology) has allowed humans to break and overcome boundaries across the world.

Human life forms persistently invent and develop new technologies to simplify daily lives and transform societies. Recent landmarks include radar tracking technology, the modern GPS systems, remote-controlled systems (drones), driverless cars, medical sensors and the possibility of discovering self-healing muscles. The world is also building a facial verification technology that is almost as accurate as the human eye.

The potential political, economic and social impact of these technological trends is profound. It is now possible to transfer power or communicate without any kind of wires. The speed, altitude and direction of a flying object can be altered simply by sending radio signals (codes) from a remote device. It is also possible to make a flying device to land using remote control.

The world has witnessed breakthrough navigational aid tools designed for visually-impaired people enabling them to move and navigate around common obstacles such as walls, chairs and staircases in a safe and easy way.

The Internet, the fastest-growing communication medium of all time, is pushing power to the edges. The Internet is literally breaking down geography. In the coming years, the Internet is going to undergo major transformations riding on mobile penetration, smart-phones, tablets, social media, online stores and digital transactions, etc. to engineer political, economic and social change. Sooner or later, domestic power plays will have to resonate with the rest of the world. Leaders are going to be elected on the basis of how effective they pursue universal values, ideals and projects.

Today the Internet is a global phenomenon. However, at first the proposal for what would become the Web was completely ignored (Gaines, 2001). The story of the Internet is traced to 1895, when Paul Otlet anticipated a universal bibliographic repository of information that could be accessed remotely from a centralized depository of interconnected computers.

However, it was not until nearly a century later in 1989 that the Internet as we know it today (the World Wide Web) started as a daring idea in a technical paper by Tim Berners-Lee, a computer scientist.

Berners-Lee's model of the Internet where people can freely publish and access what they wish on connected computer networks represents one of the several ways to facilitate sustainable connectedness.

Human beings are enjoined with the rest of the universe. The universe is goal-oriented. The object of the universe is to sustain life. The quest to sustain life manifests in experience, religion, evolution, science and change.

Human beings have come to terms with their experience, evolved, developed complex technologies and sustained change to such an unprecedented scale in the quest to prolong life.

Sometimes it's tempting to think of human beings as representing the peak of evolutionary progress. This view is, however, almost certainly false. Human beings are not special bearing in mind the first living organisms emerged from inanimate matter and on demise one becomes lifeless ceding their place on to better-adapted species. Indeed, ninety-nine percent of the species that have lived on Earth have gone extinct.

Human beings are simply thinking machines like so many others jostling to fulfill the will of the universe. Human achievements are erected on technologies fomented by the animate and inanimate thinking machines.

Technology poses unique opportunities and unusual challenges though. Some preeminent scientists such as Stephen Hawking and Max Tegmark have warned about an uncertain future where technology learns to control itself or a world where super-intelligent computers can surpass the abilities of humans.

Sadly, parochial thought processes that are premised on superiority or inferiority of one's identity have confined the world in a state of permanent competition whereas a more rational approach would be the pursuit of sustainable connectedness.

The world is staring at a crisis of values given relatedness. Human relationships tend to be characterized by mutual suspicion, backstabbing, non-cooperation, hostility and antagonism. Conflicts are everywhere: Liberia, Somalia, Central Africa Republic, the Democratic Republic of Congo, Syria, Iraq, Ukraine, Yemen, Afghanistan, Libya, Mali, Niger, Guinea Bissau, Burkina Fasso and South Sudan. This has to change.

Liberia is a pointer to what relatedness can do. The demarcation between native Liberians and the descendants of repatriated American blacks who considered themselves

Americans of Liberian descent provided room for the occurrence of dastardly incidents in the past and present-day divisions and conflicts in Liberia. The list is endless. The bottom, however, is that relatedness the wrong way to structure human relations and society.

Connectedness looks beyond the current paradigms of demarcations and borders. Connectedness involves personal identification with the rest of humanity as a cohesive whole. Sustainable connectedness is premised on a shared value system and a common goal. It is much easier to pool resources with people who concede they share a common aspiration however idiotic than to team up with a bunch of fools who suppose everything goes.

The quest for sustainable connectedness is responsible for the grand forward march of knowledge. The quest to discover the wonders of the universe has been facilitated by attempts to build bridges, surmount boundaries and bring to an end identity struggles thereby facilitate meaningful peaceful changes in the world society.

CONCEPTION OF NEW MARKETS

Productivity is driven by effective demand. The implication of this observation is that productivity and the size and level of income (employment opportunities and business contracts) are two sides of the same coin.

Long-lived perceptions hold that rural folks and those residing in slums lack purchasing power to sustain enterprise, generate quality jobs and develop the economy. Sadly, very few efforts are being expended at boosting productivity and employment generation through sensible intervention in these dispersed locations.

Against this backdrop of weak state capacity and a private sector unwilling to invest in marginal areas, the best policy approach is for the non-profit sector to increase investments in infrastructure projects in far-flung places and slums to trigger the expansion of the private sector and through that create jobs and increase tax revenues.

The plan is to mobilize goodwill funds to prop up civic investments, refocus the idle labour to bolster productivity and thereby create new markets in rural areas and slums. Simply put, to create and diversify income opportunities as well as trigger effective demand it is necessary to urbanize neighborhoods.

While the private sector (individual and private enterprise) is good at creating wealth, it is not a fair distributor of that wealth. This explains why wealth has become concentrated in a few hands and in major towns and cities the world over.

Whereas the huge populations in rural environments and slums also aspire for enhanced lifestyles, these neighborhoods remain frozen in time and prospects partly because policy debates are often shaped by urban elites with little focus on the rural spaces and slums. The net result is historical neglect, inequality, unemployment, crime and other adverse outcomes.

Urbanizing neighborhoods is the new strategy to get to the poor and to bring into the mainstream isolated remote rural places and urban slums. The nonprofit sector through Tajiriba Spaces can increase income opportunities in remote rural environments and slums by creating new markets.

Tajiriba spaces represent attempts to create new markets and make use of huge untapped opportunities existing in marginal locations through mutually beneficial arrangements.

Tajiriba spaces are shared spots within the public realm in remote and rural environments and slums that are open and accessible to all people, and that help promote social interaction and a sense of collective community.

So, Tajiriba Spaces revolves around the investment in the economically disadvantaged remote rural locations and slums throughout the world to help create new markets and diminish the meaning of borders.

The strategy is to put up commercial, office and residential facilities thereby enabling existing business brands to scale their businesses and entrepreneurs to venture into slums and remote rural neighborhoods.

This will gives rise to productivity dividends that can be used to sustain human well-being, prosperity and happiness among people of goodwill, residents, investors, manufacturers, retailers, jobseekers, innovators, thinkers, creators, entrepreneurs and policymakers, anywhere in the world.

SUSTAINABLE URBANIZATION OF NEIGHBOURHOODS

Urban centers magnify opportunities for social interaction, information exchange and step up the advance of a common value system.

Within five decades almost the entire world human population will be living in urbanized environments. In the past, urbanization has been caused by the expansion of towns and cities through rural-urban migration. However, sustainable urbanization involves mutual inflows and outflows.

Through Tajiriba Spaces it is possible to ensure that remote rural locations and slums are continually teeming with new businesses, new residents and new life.

Tajiriba Spaces seeks to introduce urban pastimes in rural environments and slums, and to provide host residents, visitors, and tourists memorable, dignified and decent living and shopping experience. The strategy is to use eco-friendly office and residential infrastructural designs to turn remote rural areas and slums into agricultural, residential and commercial urban hubs.

In the past, villages have been associated with economies of affection with rural peasant production for subsistence and simple exchange predominating. In such setups, familial, kinship, ethnic obligations or other affinities have tended to interfere with complete integration and the appreciation of the larger picture.

Shared spaces are the solution to market failures and flaws in government intervention in remote rural locations and slums. Shared spaces stem from the contemporary impulse toward the nonprofit sector for investment in infrastructure, green energy, and other civic projects.

The non-profit sector has co-existed harmoniously side by-side with the profit sector in the form of philanthropy, charity, corporate social responsibility, among other initiatives.

In the private sector, operating resources and capital investments tend to be based on the potential for payout. The non-profit sector is devoid of the profit motive such that the goods and services they deliver are more important than the potential for revenues.

The connectedness model envisages shared spaces to make it possible for governments, markets and nonprofits to coordinate and collaborate when it comes to large-scale projects requiring massive capital outlays.

The non-profit sector can partner with businesses and governments to scale up investments in persistently low-income urban and rural communities. This is a complete paradigm shift in the way governments, private for profit and nonprofit sectors are viewed.

This model represents a win-win matrix. For the private sector, this approach has the potential to shore the scope and value of existing business by a hundredfold. This is because Tajiriba Spaces are mechanisms to boost the ease of doing business in rural and remote environments and to attract and retain people with disposable income.

This approach holds a lot of promise both in terms of faster development throughout the world and decongesting the cities as more people migrate to remote and rural environments to take advantage of the opportunities created there.

OPTIMIZES THE DELIVERY OF PUBLIC AND PRIVATE GOODS AND SERVICES

Transforming peoples' lives require the building institutions and putting up the necessary infrastructure to stimulate and encourage the public and private sectors to deliver goods and services.

Despondently, the penetration and escalation of individual and private enterprise is minimal in most remote rural locations and slums since these neighborhoods are characterized by low levels of infrastructure.

Remote rural environments and slums are ripe for high-rise office blocks and apartments, hosting world-class conferences, expositions and tournaments. This can be realized when the nonprofit sector becomes involved in putting up and maintaining infrastructure.

On this score, Tajiriba Spaces are likely to optimize the delivery of goods and services in remote rural environments and slums in line with changing shopping habits and expectations.

Through Tajariba Spaces, it will be possible for the goods, services and facilities that are now only available in urban centres to be available in remote rural locations and slums.

Each Tajiriba Space would comprise office blocks, food courts, shopping malls, retail units, banking halls, accommodation facilities, car parks, fashion stores, beauty parlours, recreation facilities, book stores, libraries, residential housing units, hospitals, factories, industrial parks, learning centres, touring opportunities, conference facilities, commercial centers, social facilities, emergency shelters and burial sites. It will be possible to access goods, services and facilities under one roof.

The beauty with rural neighborhoods is that many services and amenities will be within a short walking distance. Majority of the workers would live in village apartments and other accommodation arrangements often at a walking distance to their work place.

Tajiriba Spaces are a way of devolving development and other opportunities. Each neighborhood should be able produce more goods and services for own consumption and satisfaction and to sell, exchange or donate any surpluses to other neighborhoods.

Successful and focused neighborhoods are those less interested in becoming global powers. What sustainable neighborhoods need are corridors of exchange and interaction such as hotel lobbies, restaurants, public transit systems, airports, and other interactive spaces.

Tajiriba Spaces also have the potential to transform livelihoods and improve the business environment in rural and remote locations as banks, transport and other service industries take shape.

Other benefits that can be associated with the establishment of urban systems in remote rural locations and slums include employment and tax revenues, and supportive infrastructure development through road construction, maintenance of bridges and social amenities such as education, health, sports and recreation facilities.

PROMOTING NEIGHBOURHOOD ENTERPRISES

People ought to be facilitated to interact, trade and exchange with ease. The extent of growth for neighborhood enterprises depends on the availability of infrastructure. Most rural areas which are further away from major towns and cities are impossibly underdeveloped needing to be urgently opened up for investment and urbanization. So, unless somebody comes up with the necessary infrastructure, there can only be so many income opportunities.

Startups are the engine that creates new jobs. To appreciably depopulate major towns and cities, income opportunities must be created in remote rural locations and urban slums.

Tajiriba Spaces represents the stop-gap measure in terms of the capacity for people in villages and remote locations to set up workshops and industries to fill the gaps in local markets. The nascent industries can benefit from the growth of countless small, medium-sized and big businesses in remote locations.

Neighborhood enterprises can have a multiplier effect. The first benefit will be direct jobs since most investors will be expected to source their workers locally. Very many people will be employed to run the facilities. Suppliers will also benefit from contracts, make profit and employ many more people. Demand for goods and services will facilitate entrepreneurship, trade, innovations and additional employment opportunities. There will also be need for better infrastructure to facilitate the free movement of people, capital, goods and services and to boost the bottom lines of existing and new businesses. Subsequently, more and more people will invest in remote rural areas and slums. Many entrepreneurs will get a chance to invest, hire local labour, buy local materials or sub-contract local entrepreneurs.

Tajiriba Spaces are mechanisms to expand investment and trade in remote rural environments and in slum areas. The strategy is to develop and manage commercial, office, residential and recreational infrastructural properties in these environments for lease to the public.

It may not be necessary to export commodities when people can simply consume these items right in the neighborhood after value addition. Better still, an export-led economy may sprout from the margins to co-exist with local consumption.

Tajiriba spaces are a way of driving advertisements to remote rural environments and in slum areas. Through rural ads, advertisers can target specific audiences in isolated parts of the world. Village ads can enable public places to sustain their offerings. To advertise, corporations can sponsor events and other undertakings in the villages and slums. Advertisers may also advertise on walls, bridges, pavements, store fronts and social places.

FACILITATING CREATIVITY AND INNOVATION

Creativity and innovation are functions of knowledge, curiosity and imagination; the use of imaginative and innovative ideas to come up with new and better realities, applications, products and services.

New discoveries and innovative ventures face formidable challenges in the marketplace. Remote rural neighborhoods are inhabited by creative and innovative people whose unique offerings never see the light of day.

Many start-ups have been held back because of problems in attaining funding particularly when the new ideas and innovations cannot be easily monetized.

Tajiriba Spaces are also mechanisms for nurturing and appreciating human talent, innovation and creativity in all neighborhoods around the world.

FACILITATING PERFECT EMPLOYMENT

Everybody's dream is to get an education, a steady source of income, raise a family and have enough at the end of the day for a secure retirement. Unfortunately, the huge numbers of people that are churned out on the job market outnumber the very few jobs available.

Unemployment condemns people with potential to a life of misery and raises the possibility of social disruption. Besides, because of unemployment the world economy has grown below its potential for millennia.

The dilemma the world faces is how to transform the huge human capital available to obtain a favourable outcome for the entire world.

Tajiriba Spaces represent one of the greatest single job creation drives anywhere in the world. Tajiriba Spaces will prioritize infrastructural expansion as a strategy of development and job creation. The logic is that this would spur economic growth (the efficient operation and expansion of existing businesses) thereby increasing productivity, therefore creating more jobs and other opportunities.

Each Tajiriba Space can have the capacity to offer direct employment to more than 4,000 residents of any particular neighborhood and thrice the number indirectly.

A typical neighborhood may have several homesteads and close to 2,000 people. Some neighborhoods have a population of 10,000+. The implication is that Tajiriba Spaces have the potential of lifting hundreds of millions of people out of poverty, managing rural-urban migration, and realizing zero unemployment, among other benefits.

Tajiriba Spaces are vehicles through which employment and other opportunities can be created to benefit many people around the world. The focus is to establish, maintain, and expand the private sector to cover areas particularly those that are frequently overlooked.

The nonprofit sector through Tajiriba Spaces can help create jobs and other opportunities in remote rural environments and slums, spur innovation and influence policy.

Governments benefit when people are able to work. This is because a richer populace means increased productivity and an expanded tax base. Governments will then have more resources to spend on basic services.

Tajiriba Spaces are catalysts for wider economic benefits. By uplifting neighborhoods into new urban areas, Tajiriba Spaces will help to reduce congestion, pollution, crime and the prevailing in major towns and cities.

EMPLOYER OF LAST RESORT

Many people prefer to be hired for life or until they choose to retire. Lifelong employment is a policy shift worth pursuing worldwide.

People across the world are living longer due to increased win-win scenarios, advances in health care and nutrition. However, this being an age segregated society the elderly cannot fully enjoy the happiness and fullness that comes with aging. The elderly are not a burden but a resource. Senior citizens possess extensive networks and years of experience. The elderly are often turned down by many employers preventing them from becoming relevant members of society.

Tajiriba Spaces hopes to benefit from the broad and deep knowledge the elderly have acquired from the many years in the workforce, management experience and large professional networks.

So, in pursuance of lifelong employment, Tajiriba Spaces may provide income opportunities for the elderly. Tajiriba Spaces may also avail opportunities to the long-term unemployed, people with severe disabilities, those that are talented but lack academic qualifications (i.e. artists, musicians, poets, athletes, etc), personnel who are victims of cost-cutting measures such as retrenchment or downsizing, and those in possession of unique expertise.

PROVISION OF INTERNSHIP OPPORTUNITIES

University is a time of adventure, thought and exploration. However, frequently the time at university is normally unprofitably used.

Tajiriba Spaces hopes to offer flexible opportunities for university students and fresh graduates to join the organization as volunteers and interns respectively to horn their skills.

The objective of internship is to improve the interns' employability by providing interns with work experience and skills necessary for them to find a regular job and/or start their own enterprises once they graduate.

FACILITATING PERFECT DEMOCRACY

Throughout the world, for many years, identities have determined power, economic and social relationships. The consequences have been horrendous. Forms of imperialism such as slavery, colonialism, neo-colonialism and globalization are some of the outcomes. Globalization is the most recent phase of unnecessary competition, polarity and discrimination.

The unfortunate experiences of political decay (politics relating to supremacy and victimhood, dictatorial regimes, corruption, etc.), structural limitations (state limitations, poverty and inequality, etc.) are compelling enough to necessitate the need to curve a universal path for the world.

The most promising mechanism for defusing identity struggles is to encourage detribalized non-sectarian parties to pursue inclusivity through policy prescriptions that are premised on the will of the universe rather than the more familiar will of the people (the popular will or will of the majority).

In this age, politics is more than simply a public activity that looks after the collective interests of specific identities. Besides, political parties are not mere vehicles for aspiring candidates with which to seek election. Ideally, all political parties and interest groups must be guided by the overriding resolve to sustain life. That is why it is no longer permissible to commit unspeakable gross human-rights violations in the guise of contestation for power.

The totality of human experience that encompasses slavery, colonialism and other forms of imperialism demonstrates that power is an illusion. Yet exclusive groups and individuals worldwide continue to perpetrate the most heinous crimes in pursuit of power (and resources).

Politicians have perfected the art of using notions of supremacy and pent-up grievances of their constituents to ascend to power. Nonetheless, when a tiny cadre of self-obsessed political elites persecute grievances or notions of superiority just to increase their leverage and significance they consciously or unconsciously fracture relations along fault lines.

The problem, perhaps, is due to the ambivalence of identity construction, perpetuation, endurance and the subsequent identity struggles and conflicts. That's beside the point. The human story and aspiration is to live in a free and democratic society that respects human rights and embraces universal values.

The democracy project as a process started more than 2,500 years ago. Though democracy may be universal in meaning its application has not been uniform in all cases around the world. Relatedness is the reason as to why perfect democracy remains an ideal. India with a population of approximately 1.27 billion is a democracy of repute in the world. Despite demonstrable efforts no country has achieved this goal. The failure to manage the politics relating to supremacy and victimhood is the reason imperfect democracies flood the world.

Tribalized, racist, secterian and authoritarian systems are often anchored on an insular base that is often radically biased against people perceived to be different or those who don't share their beliefs and exclusive politics. The state of affairs is more worrisome than most people would expect.

Relatedness helps to lock in voters. Politicians prefer to win elections by mobilizing blocs of voters using underhand tactics knowing they would not be hard pressed to perform.

Society develops through new ideas. Relatedness is a circumstance requiring adaptation. Regrettably, academic scholarship is clueless on this matter. And if you were to assess the mindset of a scholar (someone who should have a broader viewpoint) and an average villager on how they perceive people from other social groups (identities) you may be surprised to establish that they can't reason any differently. You know why? It is because they live the same experience. The larger picture is frequently obscured in the dominant narrative.

Ordinarily, because of relatedness, life revolves around suspicion, competition and self-interest at whichever level of identification. So, to change the dominant thought process you have to change the neighborhood. With the neighborhood (spatial location) as the fulcrum it is possible to stir the universe.

When neighborhoods embrace the beauty of a collective interest, a common value system and a shared goal that is the time the scholar and the village dweller will start imagining how humanity must in cooperation practice human rights, explore the moon, visit mars and possibly attain the will of the universe.

The inability by state units to deliver effective economic policies for inclusive growth and societal good regularly contributes to political disenfranchisement and exasperation.

The current crisis of governance arises from established political practices. Poor governance (lack of cohesion and inclusivity, authoritarian regimes, corruption, etc.) thrives on the agenda of exclusion. Therefore, the prominence of identity politics means that we are all stuck in another time.

To buttress democracy political institutions and processes worldwide must undergo tremendous transformations. Party democracy, written constitutions, judicial reviews, issue-based politics and presidential term limits must become the trend rather than the exception.

Identities have been manipulated to build walls of separation, discrimination and hatred. To rewardingly inculcate the virtue of organized life it is worthwhile to start at the neighborhood level. It is much easier to pool resources with people who concede they share a common aspiration however idiotic than to team up with a bunch of fools who suppose everything goes.

The world is global. Perfect (synergetic/inclusive) democracy is when political, legislative and judicial processes revere the universe's will (which may not necessarily be the people's will).

Perfect democracy (connectedness) requires the rise of a global citizenry pursuing a mission-driven existence.

Looking ahead, the global citizenry will continue blossoming concurrently as the percentage of the population falling into an unlisted category in terms of identity becomes the trend.

Indeed, with time as more and more people start considering themselves as non-categorized or identityless, except in terms of geography, politicians will be forced to package their policy prescriptions on the basis of a common value system and location (synergetic democracy) rather than specific communities.

MAKING NEIGHBOURHOODS PLATFORMS FOR POLICY ENGAGEMENT

Tajiriba spaces represent an innovative mechanism to enable neighborhoods to inform new knowledge and research for the purpose of influencing policymaking and policy implementation.

Science as an adaptive capacity increases the understanding of the world around us (knowledge for knowledge's sake) and also offers solutions to specific problems through theory building and sensation (observation and experiment).

Science places premium on the hunt and documentation of knowledge through experience, observation and experiments.

Universities and most academic environments over-emphasis on basic research solely conducted for information gathering. Too often, scholarly communication is also often motivated by the quest to improve biometrics and not to communicate new ideas, findings or most importantly to offer solutions. To compound matters, excessive specialization, quantification and monetization has made it difficult for the general public to access research findings.

Young scholars who attempt to curve new horizons with independent thought often attract increased attention from higher-ranking scholars not because they want to be of assistance but to put them in their place. This may mean stagnating or dropping out. The need to make it easier for scientists to work with their colleagues and residents in remote environments in non-competitive environments is urgent.

Science teaches us about life, the world, and the universe. Excessive specialization distorts reality by providing segmented information.

Connectedness is a new way to codify knowledge and share it publicly. Through Tajiriba Spaces, it is possible to tackle the entire universe, ignite public debate and include all stakeholders in coming up with resolutions to address suboptimal outcomes.

Science helps us to understand the world. Scientists have a responsibility to communicate their work with the public. Tajiriba Spaces are sites of knowledge production, dissemination and application.

Tajiriba Spaces can be avenues for the creation of new knowledge (discoveries), knowledge exchange (collaboration, sharing and communication) and applied knowledge (social change).

Tajiriba Spaces can provide platforms for dialogue dedicated to critical policy debates. Through Tajiriba Spaces it is possible to stimulate innovation, create opportunities for people to invent jobs based on their skills, influence public policies and directly improve people's lives worldwide.

Knowledge systems, discoveries and innovations along margins are capable of changing the world. Tajiriba Spaces are, therefore, mechanisms to build a tradition of knowledge and informed debate focused on policy prescriptions in remote rural environments and slums. It is an avenue for sharing life-changing ideas and experiences.

Tajiriba Places can improve the quality of contact between standout scholars and neighborhoods in terms of conferences, seminars, workshops, fieldwork, public lectures and other academic forums; provide an exciting opportunity for currently underutilized manpower; cultivate and reinforce critical and creative thinking to drive new scientific breakthroughs; scout and showcase talent for the benefit of the universe; offer people somewhere to launch startups and exploit their knowledge.

Tajiriba Spaces can facilitate the free circulation of researchers, scientific knowledge, and technology. The expectation is that relevant policy alternatives (ideas) will be offered to serve the wider interest.

The search for purpose in life is an elemental human quest. Scholars have been partisan along distinct academic fields (business, engineering, computer science, natural science and humanities) and/or along fault lines of identity.

Connectedness sums of all human knowledge. Connectedness enables us to tackle big picture questions about humanity and its prospects. Tajiriba Spaces represents the most worldwide platform for humanity to agonize over the nature of the world, the place of human beings in it and the purpose of human existence.

MAKING NEIGHBOURHOODS THE FULCRUM OF THE WORLD

The world is about to enter an era dominated by neighborhood units. One's neighborhood is simply the locality that one has the opportunity to thrive and make a difference in other peoples' lives. One's neighborhood can be the place one inhabits as in the principal residence, second home and so on. The neighborhood can also be one's home area, home town, home city or place of birth. The neighborhood can also mean the place of work, business, leisure and relaxation or anywhere special.

One's neighborhood is the geographic space one has the opportunity to thrive and touch other lives. This way of understanding neighborhoods (human contact and relations) presents a real problem when it comes to discrimination: Where do you draw the line?

At best each neighborhood should have a Tajiriba Space to act as its focal point. A typical neighborhood might have a few thousand persons or more who share a Tajiriba Space. If at all possible each Tajiriba Space should be composed of non-categorized (identityless) people pursuing the common objective of survival.

Tajiriba Spaces are meant to avoid situations where neighborhood dwellers are only those belonging to the patrilinage or common bloodlines. This coupled with the reality that neighborhood have no official boundaries is advantageous inasmuch as it reduces chances of discrimination, competition and violent conflicts.

Looking ahead, with the successful introduction of Tajiriba Spaces it will be difficult to distinguish rural residents and urban dwellers.

The neighborhood is about location, people, events and fate. The neighborhood extends worldwide corresponding to a global village. Every neighborhood anywhere in the world is part of the global village. The fact that neighborhoods are set to become increasingly important in an enjoined universe means that Tajiriba Spaces may be the path to the elusive unity of the universe.

Ideally, each Tajiriba place can act as the face of a named neighborhood. Hospitality is crucial. The genuine enthusiasm and superb visitor relations is what measures the sustainability of any neighborhood (Tajiriba Space).

Neighborhoods that are inhospitable (discriminate) attract fewer visitors, investments, resources and other opportunities. Such neighborhoods stagnate. Sustainable (successful) neighborhoods are those that encourage more contact, creativity and innovativeness, visibility and inclusiveness. Competition, tension and discrimination (common features of relatedness) are replaced with a more welcoming attitude toward new residents and visitors.

Tajiriba Spaces are conceptualized based on structures and networks across the neighborhoods constructing an alternative to the state (international) system.

Tajiriba Spaces represent as source of common ground on which to build a lasting foundation for peace, the promotion of interaction, dialogue and exchange necessary to move the universe forward.

Through good visitor relations, fairness, inclusivity, representation and participation everyone should feel at home in any neighborhood anywhere in the world.

No one should ever feel like a stranger (or foreigner) again anytime and anyplace in the world.

FACILITATING NEIGHBOURHOOD DIPLOMACY

Hans Morgenthau, Kenneth Thompson and David Clinton in *Politics Among Nations* (1948) mistakenly thought of state power in terms of self-interest. However, taking the long view, possession of military arsenal was never meant for jockeying for space and leverage.

The materialization of the state is part of the universe's evolution. The state as a spatial entity facilitates the sustenance of life within its geographical jurisdiction. Therefore, state aggression and/or expansionism violate the will of the universe.

Apparently, economic and military strengths don't translate into well-being for the average citizen. In fact, war experiences exact profound physical and emotional tolls on many troops and citizens of all stripes.

Sadly, with the emergence chemical, biological and nuclear arsenals the importance of the state (as a mechanism to sustain meaningful life) started waning.

Increasingly, war and other pursuits of justice outside the lawfully established mechanisms such as conciliation, mediation, negotiation, compensation, arbitration, adjudication, enforcement of awards and international treaties reflect regression into the rule of the jungle.

States have become predatory because the grassroots are mobilized along identities to jostle for global supremacy.

Pointedly, it is clear that the interests of the world/state elites (as in globalization) and that of the citizenry are unsustainably divergent.

It is the world citizenry's interest to pursue diplomacy, inclusiveness and connectedness. This can be achieved when individuals, organized groups and entities emerge to promote consultation, participation and collective interest.

Notable organized entities include professional associations, interest groups, NGOs, corporations, companies and states. The United Nations (UN), an international NGO, was formed to mediate the jostling among states. The UN was meant to bring about order in the state system. The International Criminal Court (ICC), an arm of the UN, is the supreme symbol of international justice. So far, the effectiveness of the UN is mixed.

The cold war was the first real test for the UN. Today it is apparent that the UN is completely at loss whenever a conflict involves the permanent members of the UN Security Council (UNSC). Besides, the reality that less powerful states are not allowed a relevant voice in global affairs undermines the legitimacy of global organizations.

The crisis in the state system shows that global governance is in a mess. Devolution is a universal trend. Worldwide decision-making is being devolved. Power, resources and functions are being devolved to the grassroots. The expectation is that increasingly decision-making will be mediated by (non-categorized) grassroots. Before long, the topmost diplomats will represent the interest of neighborhoods.

Tajiriba Spaces are an opportunity to engineer grassroots diplomacy that may render world militaries to be of no use. This way, states will lack the legitimacy and the incentives to wage unnecessary wars. The prevailing peace will see more doves taking the reign of power around the world. The hawks will either shape up or shape out.

The greatest happiness is found in positive social interactions and relationships reflecting our connectedness. People all over the world desire unity, peaceful relations and meaningful interactions. They aspire for a larger market devoid of impediments for easiness of trade, commerce and interaction. Connectedness transcends borders to capture the historically underserved.

FACILITATING NEIGHBOURHOOD MAPPING

The universe is extended infinitely in the form of spatial and non-spatial relations. In a measureless universe, geographical location in non-Euclidean space can be regarded as the center of the world.

Mapping is an important tool in efforts to penetrate remote rural areas and urban slums around the world. Remapping the world in the form of localities is the route to connectedness.

The future of the world is one characterized by the mapping of neighborhoods. Possibly each neighborhood (or Tajiriba Space) will have an Internet domain name.

Mapped neighborhoods (places) may or may not correspond to administrative units. This is on the understanding that the village is extended worldwide. It is hoped that with time the multiple types of localities that exist will blend akin a global village.

FACILITATING NEIGHBOURHOOD TOURISM

Evidently points of interaction, exchange and communication grow in leaps and bounds. Most of today's major urban centers and cities started as trading routes, markets, religious centers, administrative arenas, etc. Therefore, neighborhoods must be willing to open up to others for them to proper. They must also be willing to share their prosperity. Historically, insular successful locations became victims of their own accomplishments.

Many people all over the world desire to tour neighborhoods for hospitality, ambiance and the surrounding nature. Many people who live in rural localities and slums are hospitable and eager to welcome and even host visitors. When visitors feel welcome, tourist activity becomes a mechanism for integration not just a good business prospect or a vacation trend.

Observably, most rural and slum dwellers rarely travel. Most rural and slum dwellers have never traveled beyond their neighborhood.

Tajiriba Spaces taps on village tourism to enhance local, statewide and global integration. This can only succeed when rural and slum dwellers get the opportunity travel and sample experiences from around the world.

Tajiriba Spaces are an opportunity to engineer social change. To create an enabling environment to improve people's well being, neighborhoods must never be turned into relatedness enclaves.

The more rational approach would be to make neighborhoods less tribal and therefore attractive and prosperous through increased urbanization, industrialization, information exchange and technological innovations.

When neighborhood residents interact with people from neighboring and far-flung neighborhoods, they form lifetime relationships. Through these interactions and interchanges, they get to appreciate diverse world views, products, ideas and importance.

Through Tajiriba Spaces, it is possible render the right environment and atmosphere for people all over the world to enjoy the many scenic locations that abound in different parts of the world and that are ideal for rest, relaxation and exchange.

FACILITATING ULTIMATE CONNECTEDNESS

Connectedness is the product of a rigorous thought process. This thought process submits that evolution, experience, religion, science or simply change refers to the same reality.

Connectedness doubts the permanence of death. Ever since pre-history, the possibility of immortality has been a cause of debate. The contemplation of the prospect of our demise contributed to the evolution of funerals. The idea of God is related with the attempt to overcome bereavement. Even Jesus didn't want to die. Mourning abridges the human desire to cheat death.

Under this model, the non-spatial dimensions (e.g. gravity, senses, emotions, mental faculties, time, life and death) are simply changeable characteristics of the universe. They are all interwoven in our daily lives as we interact with the environment in an effort to stay alive.

According to connectedness, time is one of the adjustable non-physical properties of nature. The same can be said of death. The universe has existed and will exist forever.

Ray Cummings in his science fiction novel *The Girl in the Golden Atom* (1922) observed that time is what prevents all occurrences from occurring at the same time.

H.G. Wells and Paul Cook in the science fiction novel *The Time Machine* (1895) imagined a piece of equipment that can travel forwards and backwards in time.

The grandfather paradox deals with actions done in the past that can affect the future in a way that can stop the action to be done.

The ultimate desire by religious entrepreneurs, scientists and the general public is to surmount death. Jesus, the key figure in Abrahamic faiths, imagined life after death. All religions are futuristic and revolve around the attempt to overcome demise. This is also true for scientists and the general masses.

Connectedness as a thought process is premised on the understanding that the major pre-occupation of scientists is to tinker with their surroundings to prolong, preserve or make life meaningful.

Tajiriba Spaces represent another attempt by humanity to overcome relatedness in the quest to realize the ultimate connectedness.

And, as we continue mastering nature and extending our life spans, the blurred line between life and death will increasingly become unclear.

CONCLUSION

Economic growth is not enough to alleviate poverty, inequality and other sub-optimal outcomes. This write-up has demonstrated that to change the conditions under which we live and achieve sustainable development there is need to have urban settings in rural and remote areas.

Tajiriba Spaces are infrastructural platforms in remote rural environments and slum areas funded through voluntary public donations (governments, government entities and venture capitalists and investors where applicable) as a way of encouraging new investments to enhance utilization of idle labour, bolster productivity and grow the world economy.

From the foregoing illustrations, Tajiriba Spaces can be associated with many benefits. Besides, mitigating the negative impact of rural-urban migration, they are viable mechanisms for encouraging and facilitating investment in social infrastructure, human capital development and facilitating world integration.

CHAPTER FOUR

CONCLUSION

Relatedness emphasizes scarcity of resources and income opportunities. Some of the major unfavorable outcomes include discrimination, mistrust and suspicion, unemployment, poverty, economic fluctuations, global terrorism, conflicts and war.

It is however possible to restructure the world society along connectedness and to emphasize abundance of resources, income opportunities and possibilities.

Enterprise development in remote rural locations and urban slums is the solution to sub-optimal outcomes. The plan is to gradually transform marginalized and disadvantaged geographical locations into potential megacities. These require the commitment of big-scale money for a public purpose that only be raised through soliciting contributions from the public.

Though it is now widely appreciated that companies do not just exist to make a return for their shareholders, the private sector cannot afford the real estate costs associated with establishing businesses in remote rural and disadvantaged urban locations. The nonprofit sector can help the private sector to free up capital and reduce losses. Through individual and corporate philanthropy and government support it is possible to realize sustainable positive impact worldwide.

BIBLIOGRAPHY

Aristophanes. (n.d.). BrainyQuote.com. Retrieved January 1, 2015, from BrainyQuote.com Web site: http://www.brainyquote.com/quotes/quotes/a/aristophan3795 98.html.

Barbara Santa (2012). "Wealth, Power and the Future of the Planet: Four Arguments against the Extreme Concentration of Wealth". Retrieved on Saturday, December 13, 2014 from http://www.google.com/url?sa=t&rct=j&q=&esrc=s& source=web&cd=2&cad=rja&uact=8&ved=0CCYQFjAB &url=http%3A%2F%2F204.200.203.35%2Fpdf%2FIFG_ plutonomy_Part8.pdf&ei=7FeMVIbnKOn- ywPC_4CYDQ&usg=AFQjCNGxHBzXn9EsLz3_cAqp5 Eu2pKcZwQ&bvm=bv.81828268,d.bGQ

Chomsky Noam (1999). *Profit Over People: Neoliberalism and Global Order*. Seven Stories Press.

Cummings Ray (1973) [1922]. *Girl in the Golden Atom*. Hyperion Pr.

Duménil Gérard (2013). *The Crisis of Neoliberalism*. Harvard University Press.

Gaines Anne (2001). *Tim Berners-Lee and the Development of the World Wide Web (Unlocking the Secrets of Science).* Mitchell Lane Pub Inc.

Harvey David (2007) [2005]. *A Brief History of Neoliberalism.* Oxford University Press.

ILO (2014). *Global Employment Trends 2014: The Risk of a Jobless Recovery.* International Labour Organization.

ILO (2015). *World Employment and Social Outlook: Trends 2015.* International Labour Organization.

International Labor Organization (1982). "Resolution concerning statistics of the economically active population, employment, unemployment, and underemployment, adopted by the Thirteenth International Conference of Labor Statisticians". Retrieved on Saturday, December 13, 2014 from http://ilo.org/global/statistics-and-databases/standards-and-guidelines/resolutions-adopted-by-international-conferences-of-labour-statisticians/WCMS_087481/lang--en/index.htm.

Keynes, John Maynard (2011) [1936]. *The General Theory of Employment, Interest and Money.* CreateSpace Independent Publishing Platform.

Khamala Geoffreyson (2009) *Gender Dimension of Ethnic Conflicts in Kenya: The Case of Bukusu and Sabaot Communities.* MA Thesis, Kenyatta University, Kenya.

Khamala Geoffreyson (2014a). *The Perfect Theory: A Complete Unified Description of the Universe.* Tajiriba Foundation.

Khamala Geoffreyson (2014b). *What is Science! Science as an Adaptive Capacity.* Tajiriba Foundation.

Khamala Geoffreyson (2014c). *Is Science Religion.* Tajiriba Foundation.

Khamala Geoffreyson (2014d). *Wither Globalization Enter Connectedness.* Tajiriba Foundation.

Khamala Geoffreyson (2015a). *The Ultimate Theory: The Perfection Description of the Universe.* Tajiriba Foundation.

Kiernan Ben (1997). *The Pol Pot regime: Race, power and genocide in Cambodia under the Khmer Rouge, 1975–79.* New Haven, Conn: Yale University Press.

Leys Colin (1975). *Underdevelopment in Kenya, the Political Economy of Neo-Colonialism, 1964-1971.* London: Heinemann Educational Books.

Medema Steven G. (2007). "The Hesitant Hand: Mill, Sidgwick, and the Evolution of the Theory of Market Failure," *History of Political Economy*, 39(3), p p. 331-358.

Morgenthau Hans, Thompson Kenneth & Clinton David (2005) [1948]. *Politics Among Nations.* McGraw-Hill.

Orbach, Barak (2013). "What Is Government Failure," Yale Journal on Regulation Online, 30, pp. 44-56.

Renato Cirillo (1978). *The Economics of Vilfredo Pareto.* Routledge.

UN HABITAT (2007). *State of the World's Cities 2010/2011.* Nairobi: United Nations Human Settlements Programme.

UNDP Human Development Report (2014). *Sustaining Human Progress: Reducing Vulnerabilities and Building Resilience.* New York: UNDP.

United Nations (2008). *World Urbanization Prospects: The 2007 Revision Population Database.* New York: UN.

Wells H.G. and Cook Paul (2008) [1895]. *Time Machine*. Arc Manor LLC.

www.ingramcontent.com/pod-product-compliance
Lightning Source LLC
Chambersburg PA
CBHW070705290526
45790CB00001B/455